Deconstructing
The Enemy

Deconstructing The Enemy

A Path To Self-Awareness, Control, And Serenity

GEW Social Sciences & Humanities

Global East-West (London)

Copyright © 2024 by GEW Social Sciences & Humanities Team
Senior Researcher and Editor: Dr Hichem Karoui

All rights reserved. No part of this book may be reproduced in any manner whatsoever without written permission except in the case of brief quotations embodied in critical articles and reviews.

First Printing, 2024

CONTENTS

1. Introduction — 1
2. The Nature of the Enemy — 8
3. The Power of Self-Awareness — 19
4. Enemy Deconstruction — 33
5. Achieving Control and Serenity — 46
6. Application in Daily Life — 59
7. The Art of Serenity — 70
8. The Mastery of Self-Awareness — 81
9. The Path to Liberation — 94
10. The Journey Within — 107

1

Introduction

The concept of the enemy is deeply ingrained in the human psyche, shaping our perceptions, actions, and relationships in profound ways. While historically, the enemy was often a tangible threat in times of war or conflict, its definition has evolved to encompass a broader, more nuanced understanding in modern society.

At its core, the enemy represents the "other," a perceived adversary that challenges our sense of identity and belonging. This dichotomy between self and other is a fundamental aspect of human social dynamics, driving us to categorize individuals, groups, or even abstract ideas as either allies or foes. This process of "othering" can serve as a psychological defense mechanism, allowing us to simplify complex realities and justify our own beliefs and behaviors.

However, the construction of the enemy is not limited

to external threats; it also reflects internal struggles and contradictions within ourselves. Sigmund Freud's concept of the "shadow self" highlights how our repressed desires, fears, and insecurities can manifest as projected enemies in our relationships and interactions. By confronting and integrating these darker aspects of our psyche, we can cultivate a more holistic sense of self-awareness and empathy towards others.

Furthermore, the enemy is not a static or monolithic entity but a dynamic and multifaceted concept that evolves with changing social, cultural, and political contexts. In times of crisis or uncertainty, the enemy can be instrumentalized to galvanize public support, justify authoritarian measures, or fuel ideological conflicts. This instrumentalization of fear and division underscores the importance of critical thinking and ethical reflection in navigating the complexities of enemy construction.

Moreover, the enemy can also serve as a mirror through which we project our own insecurities and vulnerabilities, leading to a cycle of conflict and misunderstanding. By recognizing the ways in which we contribute to the construction of enemies through our prejudices and biases, we can begin to challenge and dismantle these harmful narratives.

The enemy, then, is not solely an external force to be conquered but a reflection of our internal landscapes and societal structures. By interrogating our assumptions, confronting our fears, and embracing the complexities of human relationships, we can begin to transcend the binary thinking that perpetuates enmity and division. In doing so, we open ourselves to a more compassionate, connected, and inclusive way of being in the world.

A. Defining the Concept of the Enemy

In order to truly understand the concept of the enemy, it is essential to delve into the various dimensions that make up this complex and often elusive idea. At its core, the enemy represents a perceived threat or obstacle that stands in opposition to one's own beliefs, values, or well-being. This adversary can take many forms - be it an individual, a group, an ideology, or even an abstract concept.

Defining the enemy requires a deep exploration of both internal and external factors that contribute to its construction. On an individual level, personal experiences, fears, biases, and insecurities can all play a role in shaping one's perception of who or what constitutes an enemy. This introspective journey involves examining one's own beliefs, attitudes, and emotions towards those deemed as adversaries.

Moreover, the societal and cultural context in which one exists also influences the understanding of the enemy. Historical events, media portrayals, and social norms all contribute to the collective construction of enemies within a given community or society. These external influences can shape perceptions and fuel animosity towards certain groups or individuals.

Psychologically, the concept of the enemy serves as a mechanism for self-preservation and identity formation. By identifying an external threat, individuals and groups can unify around a common enemy, strengthening their own sense of cohesion and purpose. This "us versus them" mentality can provide a sense of security and belonging, but it can also lead to prejudice, discrimination, and conflict.

Furthermore, the portrayal of enemies in literature, art, and media plays a crucial role in shaping cultural narratives surrounding the idea of adversaries. Through storytelling and visual representation, enemies are often depicted as villains, monsters, or evil forces that must be vanquished in order to restore balance and order. These narratives can both reflect and reinforce societal attitudes towards the "other" and perpetuate stereotypes and prejudices.

The concept of the enemy can also be seen through a political lens, where the construction of enemies is used as a tool for manipulation and control. Leaders and governments often identify external threats to rally support and justify actions that may infringe upon individual rights or lead to conflict. In this way, the enemy becomes a powerful tool for mobilizing populations and maintaining power dynamics.

In conclusion, the concept of the enemy is a multifaceted and deeply ingrained aspect of human psychology and society. By examining the internal and external factors that contribute to the construction of adversaries, we can gain a better understanding of the complexities that underlie our perceptions of enemies, and perhaps work towards fostering empathy, understanding, and peace in a world marked by division and conflict.

B. The Role of Self-Awareness in Understanding the Enemy

Understanding the enemy goes beyond surface-level characteristics or actions; it delves into the psychological constructs that shape our perceptions. Our experiences, fears, insecurities, and biases all play a role in how we define someone as an enemy. By cultivating self-awareness, we can begin to unpack the underlying factors that contribute to our construction of the enemy.

Self-awareness involves a deep understanding of oneself, including one's thoughts, emotions, motivations, and beliefs. It requires introspection and a willingness to confront the inner workings of our minds. When it comes to understanding the enemy, self-awareness helps us recognize how our own internal landscape influences our perception of others.

Through self-awareness, we can uncover hidden biases and prejudices that may color our views of the enemy. By acknowledging and challenging these ingrained beliefs, we can start to see the enemy in a more nuanced light. Self-awareness also allows us to recognize when our own actions or behaviors contribute to conflict or animosity, leading to greater accountability and introspection.

Moreover, self-awareness enables us to differentiate between legitimate threats and perceived enemies. By tuning into our emotions and reactions, we can discern whether our feelings stem from genuine danger or misguided perceptions. This clarity helps us approach the enemy with a more balanced and rational mindset, fostering empathy and understanding instead of hostility.

In essence, the role of self-awareness in understanding the enemy is pivotal. By delving into our own psyche and unraveling the complex web of influences that shape our perceptions, we can adopt a more compassionate and discerning view of the other. This inner exploration not only enriches our understanding of the enemy but also leads to greater personal growth and self-discovery.

Further examination of the psychological constructs of the enemy reveals the intricate interplay between individual experiences and societal influences. Our cultural background, upbringing, and social environment all contribute to the formation of our perceptions of the enemy. Stereotypes, media portrayals, and historical narratives can shape our attitudes towards certain groups or individuals, often leading to biases and misconceptions.

Additionally, the enemy is not a monolithic entity but a complex and multifaceted construct that varies for each individual. What one person considers as an enemy may be viewed differently by another, highlighting the subjective nature of enmity. By acknowledging the diversity of perspectives and experiences that inform our understanding of the enemy, we can move towards a more inclusive and empathetic stance.

Furthermore, the concept of the enemy is fluid and evolving, influenced by changing circumstances and personal growth. As we navigate through life, our interactions with others, the lessons we learn, and the challenges we face can reshape our perceptions of who the enemy is. This dynamic nature underscores the importance of continual self-reflection and introspection in our quest to comprehend the complexities of enmity.

In conclusion, the exploration of the psychological constructs of the enemy offers a profound insight into the intricate layers of human perception and interaction. By delving deeper into our own psyche and societal influences, we can unravel the complexities of enmity and foster a more compassionate and nuanced understanding of the other. This journey of self-discovery and empathy not only enriches our relationships with those we perceive as enemies but also holds the potential to transform our own inner landscape for the better.

* * *

2

The Nature of the Enemy

The Complex Dynamics of Enemy Perceptions

To truly grasp the nature of the enemy, one must delve into the intricate web of psychological, social, and historical factors that shape our perceptions. At the core of the concept lies a fundamental duality - the enemy as both external adversary and internal projection.

From a psychological perspective, the enemy often represents the "other" - an individual or group that is perceived as divergent from our own values, beliefs, or interests. This dichotomous distinction between "us" and "them" serves to reinforce our sense of identity and belonging within a particular group or community. In this sense, the enemy acts as a mirror through which we define ourselves and our place in the world.

Moreover, the concept of the enemy is closely tied to our innate tribal instincts, stemming from our evolutionary past as social beings. In times of conflict or competition for resources, the identification of an enemy galvanizes group cohesion and solidarity, leading to a sense of collective purpose and unity. This primal urge to rally against a common foe has profound implications for intergroup relations and conflict dynamics.

On a cultural and societal level, the construction of the enemy is often influenced by prevailing narratives, ideologies, and power dynamics. In times of war or political upheaval, the enemy is portrayed as a grave threat to national security or stability, justifying collective action and mobilization against them. This narrative construction serves to justify aggression and violence towards the perceived enemy, further perpetuating cycles of conflict and animosity.

Moreover, the enemy is not a static entity but a dynamic, ever-evolving construct that adapts to changing circumstances and contexts. Throughout history, societies have vilified different groups as enemies, from rival nations and political ideologies to religious or ethnic minorities. These shifting enemy narratives reflect the fluidity and arbitrariness of enemy perceptions, demonstrating the malleability of human conceptions of "otherness."

Exploring the deeper layers of enemy perceptions, one must also consider the role of fear, mistrust, and dehumanization in shaping attitudes towards adversaries. Fear of the unknown or unfamiliar can breed suspicion and hostility towards perceived enemies, leading to exaggerated threats and a distorted view of their intentions. This fear-driven mindset can fuel conflict escalation and perpetuate cycles of violence and retribution.

Furthermore, the dehumanization of the enemy is a common psychological mechanism used to justify acts of aggression and violence. By depicting the enemy as less than human, devoid of empathy or moral worth, individuals can rationalize their hostile actions and minimize feelings of guilt or remorse. This dehumanizing rhetoric not only perpetuates stereotypes and prejudice but also hinders efforts towards reconciliation and peacebuilding.

In essence, the complex dynamics of enemy perceptions reveal the intricate interplay of individual, social, and historical factors that shape our attitudes towards adversaries. By acknowledging the multidimensional nature of the enemy, we can begin to deconstruct harmful stereotypes and prejudices, fostering a more nuanced understanding of conflict and promoting empathy and mutual respect across perceived divides.

A. Exploring the Psychological Constructs of the Enemy

In exploring the psychological constructs of the enemy, we delve into the intricate web of perceptions, biases, and underlying motivations that shape our understanding of who the enemy is. The enemy is not just an external entity but a complex interplay of our own beliefs, fears, and insecurities projected onto others.

Psychologically, the enemy serves as a convenient scapegoat onto which we can offload our own unresolved issues and emotions. By attributing negative traits or intentions to the enemy, we create a dichotomy between "us" and "them" that reinforces our own sense of identity and belonging. This process of "othering" can be deeply ingrained in our psyche, rooted in primal instincts of tribalism and survival.

Moreover, our perception of the enemy is often shaped by cognitive biases such as confirmation bias, where we seek out information that confirms our preconceived notions, and attribution bias, where we attribute negative actions to the inherent nature of the enemy while explaining away their positive actions as exceptions.

Additionally, societal and cultural influences play a significant role in defining who we perceive as the enemy. Media portrayal, historical narratives, and political rhetoric all contribute to shaping our views of those deemed as threats to our well-being or values. These external influences can reinforce stereotypes, fuel prejudice, and perpetuate cycles of animosity.

Furthermore, the concept of the enemy can be deeply intertwined with our sense of self-preservation and group identity. Evolutionarily, humans have been wired to distinguish between ingroups (those perceived as similar to us) and outgroups (those perceived as different or threatening). This division has helped our ancestors survive in a hostile world but can also lead to harmful social dynamics and conflicts when taken to extremes.

Examining the psychological constructs of the enemy requires a willingness to confront our own shadow selves – the parts of us that we may not want to acknowledge or accept.

By shining a light on these dark corners of our psyche, we can begin to understand how our perceptions of the enemy are often projections of our own fears, insecurities, and unhealed wounds.

In breaking down the barriers that separate us from those we label as enemies, we open up space for empathy, compassion, and ultimately, reconciliation. By recognizing the interconnectedness of all beings and the universal human desire for understanding and connection, we can transcend the limitations of enemy narratives and move towards a more harmonious and peaceful coexistence.

Delving deeper into the complexities of enemy constructs, we must acknowledge the role of power dynamics in shaping our relationships with perceived adversaries. The enemy is not always a faceless, nameless entity but can often represent systemic injustices, historical grievances, and imbalances of power that fuel cycles of conflict and oppression.

On an individual level, the enemy can also manifest as a projection of our own internal struggles and unresolved traumas. When we demonize others as enemies, we may be avoiding confronting our own shadows and facing the discomfort of introspection. By externalizing our fears and insecurities onto external targets, we create a distorted narrative that perpetuates division and animosity.

Moreover, the concept of the enemy is not static but evolves with changing circumstances, narratives, and perceptions. What may have been perceived as an enemy in one context could shift to an ally or neutral party in another context. Our understanding of who the enemy is can be shaped by evolving dialogues, shared experiences, and increased empathy towards those we once labeled as adversaries.

In essence, the construct of the enemy is a multifaceted phenomenon that reflects the intricacies of human psychology, societal dynamics, and power structures. By delving into the complexities of enemy narratives, we can begin to unravel the threads of fear, prejudice, and division that separate us from others and move towards a more nuanced and holistic understanding of human relationships and conflicts.

B. Societal and Cultural Influences on Perceiving Enemies

The complexity of how individuals perceive their enemies is deeply intertwined with the fabric of our societies and cultures, shaped by a multitude of factors that extend beyond individual experiences. Exploring the societal and cultural influences on enemy constructs is essential in understanding the intricate dynamics at play in human relationships and conflicts.

Societal structures and institutions wield substantial influence in shaping our perceptions of enemies. The media, as a powerful agent of influence, plays a pivotal role in sculpting public opinions and constructing narratives around who embodies the role of the adversary. By framing certain groups or individuals as threats through news coverage, movies, and other forms of media, stereotypes and biases are reinforced, permeating societal consciousness and influencing how enemies are perceived. Furthermore, political rhetoric can intensify these perceptions, polarizing communities and fostering an environment of division and animosity.

Delving into historical narratives reveals the enduring impact of past conflicts and injustices on our understanding of enemies. Legacy narratives from wars, colonization, and other historical traumas can wield a lasting influence on intergroup relations, perpetuating cycles of hostility and prejudice. The collective memory of these grievances passed down through generations can fuel deep-seated animosities and solidify entrenched divisions between individuals and communities. Understanding the historical context in which enemy perceptions are formed is essential in deconstructing these biases and working towards reconciliation.

Cultural beliefs and values also play a significant role in shaping enemy constructs. Cultural norms surrounding identity, power dynamics, and conflict resolution can profoundly impact how adversaries are defined within a society. The boundaries of who is considered an enemy may vary across cultures, influenced by values of collectivism, individualism, loyalty, and morality. These cultural intricacies shape the framing and resolution of conflicts, shaping how enemies are perceived within different cultural contexts.

Intergroup dynamics and stereotypes further contribute to the complexity of enemy perceptions within societal and cultural frameworks. Biases and prejudices ingrained through socialization processes can lead to the categorization of certain groups as adversaries based on perceived differences or misunderstandings. Stereotypes and preconceived notions regarding social groups or ethnicities can heighten tensions and perpetuate the us vs. them mentality, exacerbating conflicts and hindering understanding between individuals and communities.

Recognizing and critically examining the societal and cultural influences on enemy constructs is essential in fostering a more inclusive and empathetic society. By addressing biases, stereotypes, and historical traumas, individuals can work towards overcoming divisions and building bridges towards reconciliation and understanding with those they perceive as adversaries.

C. Historical Perspectives on the Concept of the Enemy

As civilizations continued to evolve, so too did the dynamics of enmity. The concept of the enemy became increasingly intertwined with notions of identity and belonging, shaping not only political and military conflicts but also cultural and social divisions. In many cases, the enemy served as a convenient scapegoat for internal grievances and tensions, allowing rulers and leaders to rally their people around a common foe and deflect attention away from domestic challenges.

The enemy was not always a monolithic entity but could take on multiple forms depending on the context and interests of those defining it. In times of war, the enemy was often portrayed as a faceless mass of adversaries, dehumanized and demonized to justify acts of violence and aggression. Propaganda and rhetoric played a crucial role in shaping public perceptions of the enemy, reinforcing stereotypes and prejudices that served to justify and perpetuate conflict.

At the same time, the concept of the enemy was also a source of moral and existential reflection. Philosophers and thinkers throughout history grappled with the implications of enmity, pondering questions of justice, ethics, and the nature of human relationships. Some argued that the enemy was a necessary foil, a contrast against which one's own values and beliefs could be defined and reaffirmed. Others believed that the enemy was a reflection of one's own fears and insecurities, a projection of internal conflicts onto external adversaries.

In the modern era, the concept of the enemy has taken on new dimensions in the age of information and connectivity. The digital realm has become a battleground where competing narratives and ideologies vie for dominance, blurring the line between friend and foe. Social media platforms amplify and magnify the voices of both allies and adversaries, creating echo chambers and polarizing communities in ways previously unseen.

The enemy, therefore, is no longer a static and fixed entity but a dynamic and fluid construct that evolves and mutates in response to changing circumstances and perspectives. To confront the enemy is to engage in a complex dance of power, identity, and ideology, navigating the shifting currents of conflict and cooperation in a world that is both interconnected and fragmented.

By probing the depths of historical perspectives on the concept of the enemy, we gain a deeper understanding of the intricate web of relationships and tensions that define human societies. The enemy, in all its incarnations and complexities, remains a potent force that shapes our collective destinies and challenges us to confront our deepest fears and prejudices with courage and empathy.

* * *

Bibliography

Emile, Bruneau., Nour, Kteily. (2017). The enemy as animal: Symmetric dehumanization during asymmetric warfare.. PLOS ONE, doi: 10.1371/JOURNAL.PONE.0181422

Fellman, Gordon. "Enemy, Concept and Identity Of." Elsevier EBooks, January 1, 2022, 68–75. https://doi.org/10.1016/b978-0-12-820195-4.00210-7.

H. Shmuel Erlich. "Enemies within and Without: Paranoia and Regression in Groups and Organizations." Routledge EBooks, May 30, 2018, 115–31. https://doi.org/10.4324/9780429483387-6.

Jeffrey, Stevenson, Murer. (2009). Constructing the enemy-other: Anxiety, trauma and mourning in the narratives of political conflict. Psychoanalysis, Culture and Society, doi: 10.1057/PCS.2008.33

Lily, Gurton-Wachter. (2009). "An Enemy, I suppose, that Nature has made": Charlotte Smith and the natural enemy. European Romantic Review, doi: 10.1080/10509580902840475

Marcus, Schulzke. (2012). Creating an Enemy: Social Militarization in the War on Terror. Canadian Political Science Review,

Maxine, Sheets-Johnstone. (2010). The enemy: a twenty-first century archetypal study. Psychotherapy and Politics International, doi: 10.1002/PPI.220

Michener, Willa. "The Individual Psychology of Group Hate." Journal of Hate Studies 10, no. 1 (January 1, 2012): 15. https://doi.org/10.33972/jhs.112.

Noelia, Hernando-Real. (2022). Enemies. The Eugene O'Neill review, doi: 10.5325/eugeoneirevi.43.1.0102

Rosemary, Gordon, Montagnon. (2005). 'Do be my enemy for friendship's sake' (Blake).. Journal of Analytical Psychology, doi: 10.1111/J.0021-8774.2005.00507.X

Zhang, Wen. (2022). Enemy, Concept and Identity of. doi: 10.1016/b978-0-12-820195-4.00210-7

3

The Power of Self-Awareness

The Power of Vulnerability in Transforming Perception

Delving deeper into the intricate tapestry of vulnerability and its profound impact on our perception of the enemy, we uncover the transformative power it holds within our hearts and minds. In a world where strength is often equated with stoicism and unwavering fortitude, vulnerability emerges as a beacon of authenticity and emotional resonance that can bridge the chasm between adversaries.

At its core, vulnerability speaks to our shared humanity, reminding us that beneath the façade of conflict and animosity lie individuals with their own dreams, fears, and vulnerabilities. By embracing our own vulnerabilities, we not only cultivate empathy and compassion but also recognize the vulnerability inherent in our perceived enemies. This realization shatters the illusion of 'otherness,' revealing the common threads of vulnerability that bind us together in the tapestry of humanity.

Furthermore, vulnerability enables us to peel back the layers of emotional armor that shield us from the discomfort of confronting our biases and prejudices. In exposing our vulnerabilities, we open ourselves up to the raw and unfiltered truths that lie beneath the surface, inviting introspection and self-awareness. This process of self-discovery allows us to unravel the tangled web of assumptions and preconceptions that cloud our perception of the enemy, paving the way for a more nuanced and empathetic engagement.

Moreover, vulnerability serves as a catalyst for genuine connection and intimacy, fostering a sense of openness and trust that transcends the barriers of fear and defensiveness. When we embrace vulnerability in our interactions with the enemy, we create a space for authentic dialogue and mutual understanding to take root. This vulnerability-infused engagement lays the foundation for empathy to flourish, deepening our capacity to see beyond the masks of hostility and uncover the underlying humanity that unites us all.

In essence, the journey towards understanding the enemy through the lens of vulnerability is a transformative odyssey that calls upon us to embrace the complexity of our emotions, vulnerabilities, and biases. By courageously embracing vulnerability and extending empathy towards the perceived 'other,' we embark on a path of reconciliation, healing, and interconnectedness that transcends the confines of enmity. Through the alchemy of vulnerability and empathy, we sow the seeds of understanding and compassion, fostering a world where differences are celebrated, and unity prevails in the face of discord and division.

A. Understanding the Self: Key Concepts and Techniques

To truly understand the self, one must first delve into the core concepts and techniques that underlie this process. Self-awareness is the foundation upon which all inner exploration is built. It involves an honest and objective introspection into one's thoughts, emotions, beliefs, and behaviors.

Key concepts such as self-reflection, self-acceptance, and self-compassion play a crucial role in understanding the self. Self-reflection involves a systematic examination of one's thoughts and actions, aiming to uncover patterns and motivations behind them. It allows for a deeper insight into one's values, desires, and fears.

Self-acceptance is the acknowledgment and embracing of all aspects of oneself, including the qualities and flaws. It involves letting go of self-judgment and criticism, fostering a sense of worthiness and self-love. Self-compassion, on the other hand, involves treating oneself with kindness and understanding, especially in times of struggle and suffering.

Techniques such as journaling, meditation, and therapy can aid in the journey of self-understanding. Journaling allows for the externalization of one's internal dialogue, providing insights into one's innermost thoughts and feelings. Meditation cultivates mindfulness and presence, helping individuals connect with their inner selves and observe their thoughts without attachment. Therapy offers a safe space for exploring deeper issues and patterns, guided by a professional trained in facilitating self-discovery.

When delving into self-awareness, it is important to examine one's core beliefs and narratives that shape their identity. These beliefs are often formed in early childhood and can unconsciously influence one's thoughts, emotions, and behaviors throughout life. By bringing these beliefs to light and challenging their validity, individuals can gain a clearer understanding of themselves and make conscious choices aligned with their authentic self.

Practicing self-compassion involves treating oneself with the same kindness and understanding that one would offer to a close friend. This mindset shift can transform the way individuals relate to themselves, fostering greater self-esteem and resilience in the face of challenges. Self-compassion also includes acknowledging and validating one's emotions, allowing for a greater sense of emotional well-being and inner peace.

In embracing self-acceptance, individuals must cultivate a sense of unconditional love and respect for themselves, regardless of their perceived shortcomings or failures. This process involves releasing the need for external validation and instead finding validation from within. By accepting all parts of oneself, even the aspects that may be difficult or uncomfortable, individuals can experience a profound sense of wholeness and authenticity.

Through the ongoing practice of self-awareness, self-reflection, self-acceptance, and self-compassion, individuals can embark on a transformative journey of self-discovery and personal growth. This journey requires courage, vulnerability, and a willingness to confront the depths of one's being. By embracing the complexity and beauty of the self, individuals can uncover their true essence and live a life of purpose, authenticity, and fulfillment.

B. Examining Cognitive Biases and Their Impact on Enemy Construction

In understanding the construction of enemies, it is crucial to delve deeper into the role of cognitive biases in shaping our perceptions and judgments. Cognitive biases are inherent in the human psyche, representing systematic patterns of deviation from rationality that can profoundly influence how we view and interact with others. By exploring these biases in the context of enemy construction, we gain insight into the complexities underlying our attitudes and behaviors towards those we consider adversaries.

Confirmation bias, a prevalent cognitive bias, plays a significant role in solidifying enemy constructs. This bias predisposes us to selectively seek out information that aligns with our preconceived beliefs and values while disregarding contradictory evidence. When applied to the formation of enemies, confirmation bias reinforces our negative perceptions by amplifying instances that validate our views and overlooking nuances that may challenge them. By actively recognizing and counteracting confirmation bias, we can begin to peel back the layers of bias that cloud our understanding of others.

The fundamental attribution error adds another layer of complexity to enemy construction by influencing how we attribute motives and intentions to individuals deemed as adversaries. This bias inclines us to overemphasize internal factors, such as personality traits or inherent characteristics, in explaining others' behavior while disregarding external influences or situational contexts. When applied to enemies, the fundamental attribution error can lead to a one-dimensional portrayal of individuals as solely driven by negative intentions, disregarding the intricate interplay of factors that contribute to their actions. By challenging this bias and considering the broader spectrum of influences shaping behavior, we can foster a more empathetic and nuanced perspective on those we perceive as enemies.

The availability heuristic, a cognitive bias rooted in the ease with which information comes to mind, further complicates the construction of enemies. This bias causes us to overestimate the significance of easily recalled negative experiences or information, leading to an exaggeration of the threat posed by individuals or groups we perceive as adversaries. The availability heuristic fosters a skewed perception that prioritizes negative aspects while downplaying positive elements when constructing enemy narratives. By consciously engaging with this bias and broadening our sources of information, we can mitigate its impact on enemy construction and approach others with a more balanced perspective.

Furthermore, the negativity bias, a cognitive predisposition to prioritize negative stimuli over positive ones, shapes how we perceive and interpret the actions of others, especially those categorized as enemies. This bias heightens our sensitivity to perceived threats or negative traits in individuals, contributing to an exaggerated perception of their harmful intent or malevolence. By acknowledging the influence of the negativity bias on enemy construction, we can strive to adopt a more balanced and comprehensive view of others, recognizing the diversity of their characteristics and motivations beyond the lens of negativity.

In unraveling the intricate web of cognitive biases that underpin enemy construction, we can embark on a journey towards greater empathy, understanding, and reconciliation with those we once viewed as adversaries. By interrogating our biases, challenging our assumptions, and embracing the complexity of human nature, we can transcend the limitations of simplistic enemy narratives and forge connections rooted in compassion and mutual respect.

Delving further into these cognitive biases reveals a deeper understanding of how our minds construct enemies. Confirmation bias, for instance, not only influences how we search for information but also affects how we interpret and remember information. This bias can subtly reinforce our negative perceptions over time, as we repeatedly expose ourselves only to information that confirms our existing beliefs about our enemies. This reinforcement can result in a self-perpetuating cycle of bias that makes it even harder to break down these negative perceptions and see our adversaries in a more nuanced light.

The fundamental attribution error, on the other hand, highlights the tendency to overlook situational factors when judging others. When it comes to enemies, this bias can lead us to attribute their actions solely to their character or intentions, ignoring the complexities of their circumstances and the broader context in which they operate. By recognizing and challenging this bias, we open ourselves up to a more holistic understanding of those we perceive as enemies, acknowledging the interplay of internal and external factors that shape their behavior.

Additionally, the availability heuristic serves as a reminder of the power of salient information in shaping our perceptions. The ease with which negative information comes to mind can heavily influence how we see our enemies, often exaggerating their negative traits and downplaying any positive aspects. This bias can create a skewed and imbalanced view of others, fueling animosity and prejudice. By actively seeking out diverse sources of information and consciously working to overcome the pull of the availability heuristic, we can cultivate a more nuanced and empathetic perspective towards those we view as adversaries.

Moreover, the negativity bias underscores the greater weight we give to negative experiences and information compared to positive ones. This inclination can lead us to focus disproportionately on the harmful or threatening aspects of our enemies, overlooking their humanity and potential for positive engagement. By recognizing the influence of this bias and consciously shifting our attention towards a more balanced view, we can begin to break down the barriers that separate us from those we perceive as enemies, fostering possibilities for understanding and reconciliation.

In reflecting on these cognitive biases and their impact on enemy construction, we can strive towards a more compassionate and inclusive approach to how we view and engage with others. By actively challenging our biases, broadening our perspectives, and embracing the complexity of human nature, we can begin to dismantle the rigid boundaries that separate us from those we designate as adversaries, opening up pathways for dialogue, empathy, and ultimately, peace.

C. Self-Reflection and its Role in Deconstructing Enemy Constructs

Self-reflection is a profound and essential practice that holds the power to deconstruct even the most entrenched enemy constructs within our minds and society. It is a process that requires delving deep into the recesses of our psyche, bravely facing our innermost fears, biases, and insecurities. As we navigate this internal landscape, we begin to uncover the intricate web of experiences and conditioning that have shaped our perceptions of others as enemies.

Through self-reflection, we gain insight into the emotional triggers and thought patterns that influence our interactions with those we perceive as adversaries. By shining a light on these ingrained beliefs and reactions, we can start to dismantle the walls of separation that divide us from one another. This intimate exploration allows us to cultivate compassion and empathy for both ourselves and those we once labeled as enemies, recognizing the shared humanity and interconnectedness that unites us all.

In the depths of self-reflection, we also come face to face with our own capacity for harm and prejudice. Confronting the shadow aspects of our psyche requires courage and humility, as we acknowledge the ways in which we have contributed to the perpetuation of enemy constructs. By taking ownership of our role in this cycle of division and violence, we open the door to transformation and reconciliation.

As we journey inward with sincerity and openness, we begin to unravel the complex tapestry of beliefs and perceptions that have shaped our worldview. Through this process of unraveling, we make space for new understandings to emerge, challenging and reshaping our preconceived notions about who our enemies truly are. In this space of introspection and growth, we find the possibility of healing and reconciliation, both within ourselves and in our relationships with others.

Self-reflection, then, becomes not just a personal practice but a revolutionary act of dismantling the enemy constructs that perpetuate harm and division in our world. It is through this deep and courageous exploration of the self that we can pave a path towards peace, understanding, and unity, transcending the artificial boundaries that separate us and embracing the inherent interconnectedness of all beings.

Embracing the depth of self-reflection also involves acknowledging the unseen influences that shape our perceptions and interactions. These influences can stem from societal norms, cultural conditioning, historical contexts, and personal experiences. By examining these layers of influence, we gain a deeper understanding of how our beliefs and biases have been shaped and reinforced over time.

Furthermore, self-reflection invites us to challenge our assumptions and question the narratives that we have internalized about who our enemies are and why they exist. It requires us to move beyond surface-level judgments and stereotypes, delving into the complexities of human nature and the multifaceted dynamics that underpin conflicts and divisions.

Through this extended journey of self-discovery and introspection, we come to realize that the boundaries between "us" and "them" are not as rigid as they may seem. We begin to see the interconnectedness of all living beings and the universal experiences of joy, suffering, and longing that unite us at a fundamental level.

As we continue to navigate the depths of self-reflection, we find ourselves on a path of transformation and growth, shedding old paradigms of division and embracing a more holistic perspective that honors the inherent worth and dignity of every individual. In this process, we not only heal the wounds of separation within ourselves but also sow the seeds of empathy, understanding, and reconciliation in our relationships with others.

* * *

Bibliography

(2023). Self-awareness in the process of redemption from nathaniel hawthorne's the scarlet letter (1850) and graham greene's the power and the glory (1940). doi: 10.36106/ijar/2319797

Aaron, T., Beck. (2016). The Self in Understanding and Treating Psychological Disorders.

Ahmad, Idris, Asmaradhani. (2019). Enemy Construction in the Declaration of War against Japanese Empire: CDA Perspective. doi: 10.15642/NOBEL.2019.10.2.117-130

Brett, Silverstein., Catherine, Flamenbaum. (1989). Biases in the Perception and Cognition of the Actions of Enemies. Journal of Social Issues, doi: 10.1111/J.1540-4560.1989.TB01542.X

Brigitte, Naderer., Diane, K., Rieger., Ulrike, Schwertberger. (2023). An online world of bias. The mediating role of cognitive biases on extremist attitudes. Communications, doi: 10.1515/commun-2021-0115

Bromley, Helen, and Summan Rasib. "Understanding Yourself." Routledge EBooks, November 8, 2022, 41–53. https://doi.org/10.4324/9781003191087-5.

Ceren, Bengu, Cibik., Daniel, Sgroi. (2020). The effect of self-awareness on dishonesty.

Christian, Onof. (2013). Sartre's understanding of the self. doi: 10.4324/9781315729695-11

Christine, Crone. (2020). Al-Mayadeen: The Construction of an Enemy Image. Global media journal, doi: 10.22032/DBT.44935

Ed, Bukszar. (2009). Strategic Bias: The Impact of Cognitive Biases on Strategy. Canadian Journal of Administrative Sciences-revue Canadienne Des Sciences De L Administration, doi: 10.1111/J.1936-4490.1999.TB00617.X

Eleanor, Stein. (2007). Construction of an Enemy. Monthly Review, doi: 10.14452/MR-055-03-2003-07_12

Keyao, Li., Sai, On, Cheung. (2019). Unveiling Cognitive Biases in Construction Project Dispute Resolution through the Lenses of Third-Party Neutrals. Journal of Construction Engineering and Management-asce, doi: 10.1061/(ASCE)CO.1943-7862.0001707

Murer, Jeffrey Stevenson. "Constructing the Enemy-Other: Anxiety, Trauma and Mourning in the Narratives of Political Conflict." Psychoanalysis, Culture & Society 14, no. 2 (June 24, 2009): 109–30. https://doi.org/10.1057/pcs.2008.33.

Mustokova, Sitora, Umurzokovna,, Khaydarova, Nodirabegim, Ahtamjonovna. (2022). Self-Awareness. doi: 10.4324/9781003276852-3

Nikil, Dutt., Carlo, S., Regazzoni., Bernhard, Rinner., Xin, Yao. (2020). Self-Awareness for Autonomous Systems. doi: 10.1109/JPROC.2020.2990784

RonNell, Anderson, Jones., Lisa, Grow, Sun. (2017). Enemy Construction and the Press. Social Science Research Network, doi: 10.2139/SSRN.2929708

Saeed, Shoja, Shafti. (2018). Self-understanding: An analytic End-result of Self-absorption. International Journal of Psychoanalysis and Education.

Shane, M., O'Mara. (2018). The Importance of Cognitive Biases. doi: 10.1007/978-3-319-49154-7_5

Shihui, Han., Georg, Northoff. (2009). Understanding the self: a cultural neuroscience approach. Progress in Brain Research, doi: 10.1016/S0079-6123(09)17814-7

Tanya, Basok., Danièle, Bélanger., Martha, Luz, Rojas, Wiesner., Guillermo, Candiz. (2015). Techniques of the Self in the Face of Precarity. doi: 10.1057/9781137509758_4

Wenqian, Zhang. (2023). A Study of Self-awareness in the Power of the Dog with Lacan Theory. Communications in Humanities Research, doi: 10.54254/2753-7064/3/20220348

4

Enemy Deconstruction

The Art of Deconstructing the Enemy

In the intricate tapestry of human interactions, the construction of the enemy is a deeply ingrained phenomenon that shapes our thoughts, emotions, and behaviors in profound ways. To deconstruct the enemy is to unravel the layers of misconceptions, biases, and stereotypes that obscure our understanding of others. It is a profound exercise in self-reflection and empathy, requiring us to confront our own internalized narratives and challenge the status quo of adversarial relationships.

At the core of deconstructing the enemy lies the recognition of the inherent humanity that exists in all individuals, even those we perceive as adversaries. By delving beneath the surface of surface-level differences and societal constructs, we can begin to uncover the common threads that bind us together as human beings. This process of humanization is essential in bridging the divide between "us" and "them" and fostering a sense of interconnectedness and shared humanity.

Empathy, the ability to understand and share the feelings of another, plays a central role in the deconstruction of the enemy. By cultivating a genuine sense of empathy towards those we perceive as enemies, we open ourselves up to new perspectives and insights that challenge our preconceived notions. Through empathetic engagement, we can build bridges of understanding and compassion that transcend the boundaries of fear and distrust.

Perspective-taking is another crucial element in deconstructing the enemy. By stepping outside of our own subjective viewpoint and attempting to see the world through the eyes of the perceived adversary, we can gain valuable insights into their motivations, fears, and struggles. This act of perspective-taking allows us to uncover the complex web of factors that contribute to the enemy construct and enables us to approach them with a more nuanced and compassionate perspective.

Deconstructing the enemy also requires a willingness to engage in uncomfortable conversations and confront the realities of power dynamics that underpin adversarial relationships. Power, in its various forms, influences how we perceive and interact with others, often shaping our perceptions and actions in subtle ways. By interrogating the role of power in our relationships with enemies, we can uncover the structural inequalities and injustices that perpetuate division and promote othering.

Furthermore, the process of deconstructing the enemy

necessitates a commitment to ongoing self-reflection and personal growth. It is not a one-time task but a continuous journey of exploration and discovery. By embracing the discomfort of challenging our own beliefs and confronting our biases, we can move towards a more profound understanding of ourselves and others. Through this process of self-examination, we can cultivate greater empathy, compassion, and connection with those we once considered enemies.

In essence, the art of deconstructing the enemy is a transformative journey towards greater empathy, understanding, and unity. It challenges us to look beyond the surface of adversarial relationships and confront the complexities of human nature. By dismantling the walls that divide us and embracing the inherent humanity in all individuals, we can forge a path towards a more peaceful and inclusive world where differences are celebrated and unity is embraced.

A. Identifying and Challenging Assumptions about the Enemy

In this chapter, we delve into the complexities of identifying and challenging assumptions about the concept of the enemy. It is crucial to recognize that our perceptions and beliefs about who or what constitutes an enemy are often shaped by a myriad of factors, including our upbringing, societal influences, personal experiences, and cognitive biases.

One of the key steps in deconstructing the enemy is to critically examine the assumptions we hold about them. This involves questioning the validity and origins of these assumptions, as well as considering the possibility that they may be based on faulty reasoning or misconceptions.

Our assumptions about the enemy are not formed in a vacuum. They are influenced by a complex interplay of historical narratives, media portrayals, cultural norms, and individual experiences. These narratives often serve to reinforce stereotypes and perpetuate division, making it all the more important to interrogate and challenge them.

When we take the time to peel back the layers of our assumptions and biases, we begin to unearth a more nuanced and multifaceted understanding of the so-called enemy. We come to realize that behind the labels and preconceived notions lies a complex tapestry of human experiences, emotions, and aspirations.

By confronting our assumptions about the enemy, we open ourselves up to a profound shift in perspective—a shift that allows us to see beyond the surface-level differences and recognize the humanity that we all share. This newfound empathy and understanding can serve as a powerful catalyst for healing and reconciliation in the face of conflict and animosity.

Moreover, challenging our assumptions about the enemy requires us to cultivate a sense of humility and introspection. It demands that we acknowledge our own role in perpetuating misunderstandings and biases, and commit to actively seeking out alternative viewpoints and narratives.

In dismantling our assumptions about the enemy, we not only dismantle the barriers that separate us but also lay the groundwork for a more inclusive and interconnected world. It is through this process of self-reflection and critical

DECONSTRUCTING THE ENEMY

engagement that we can begin to bridge divides, foster empathy, and shape a more peaceful and harmonious future for all.

By engaging in conversations with those we perceive as enemies, we often discover common ground and shared values that transcend our differences. This recognition of our shared humanity is a powerful tool for building bridges and finding pathways to peace.

It is important to understand that the notion of the enemy is not fixed or immutable. It is a construct that can be deconstructed and reimagined. By challenging our assumptions and biases, we create space for new narratives to emerge—narratives that are grounded in understanding, empathy, and mutual respect.

Ultimately, the process of confronting and challenging our assumptions about the enemy is a deeply transformative one. It requires us to confront our own fears and prejudices, to listen with an open heart and mind, and to commit to building a more inclusive and compassionate world.

In the journey toward dismantling the enemy, we not only free ourselves from the constraints of division and hostility but also pave the way for a future defined by connection, understanding, and unity. It is through this profound act of courage and compassion that we can truly begin to transcend the limitations of prejudice and forge a path toward a more peaceful and harmonious coexistence.

B. Empathy and Perspective-Taking in Enemy Deconstruction

Exploring empathy and perspective-taking is crucial in the deconstruction of perceived enemies. It is a dynamic process that requires openness, curiosity, and a willingness to challenge our preconceived notions. Empathy is the ability to understand and share the feelings of another, to see the world through their eyes and connect with their humanity. By practicing empathy, we can break down the walls of separation that divide us and begin to recognize the common threads that bind us together.

Perspective-taking goes hand in hand with empathy, as it involves stepping outside of our own worldview and considering alternative viewpoints. This requires a conscious effort to suspend judgment, listen actively, and seek to understand rather than simply react. Perspective-taking allows us to see the complexities of human experience, the nuances of individual narratives, and the underlying factors that shape people's beliefs and behaviors.

Active listening is a powerful tool for fostering empathy and perspective-taking. It involves giving our full attention to the speaker, seeking to understand their words, emotions, and underlying messages. Through active listening, we can cultivate deeper connections, build trust, and create space for authentic dialogue and mutual understanding.

Engaging in dialogue with perceived enemies can be a transformative experience. By approaching these conversations with an open heart and mind, we create opportunities for empathy to flourish and for barriers to be broken down.

Through respectful communication and a genuine willingness to listen and learn, we can begin to unravel the layers of misunderstanding and mistrust that fuel conflict.

In the journey towards deconstructing enemies, empathy and perspective-taking are our guiding lights. They illuminate the path towards reconciliation, healing, and unity, reminding us of our shared humanity and capacity for compassion. By embracing empathy and perspective-taking, we embrace the power of connection, empathy, and understanding in the face of adversity.

To truly deconstruct perceived enemies, we must also acknowledge the role of power dynamics, history, and systemic injustices in shaping our perceptions and relationships. Recognizing the impact of privilege, oppression, and historical traumas is essential in fostering genuine empathy and dismantling harmful stereotypes and biases. By confronting these uncomfortable truths and engaging in critical self-reflection, we can deepen our understanding of the complexities at play and work towards creating a more just and equitable world for all.

Furthermore, drawing upon principles of restorative justice and conflict resolution can provide valuable frameworks for transforming adversarial relationships into opportunities for healing and reconciliation. By centering the needs and experiences of all parties involved, we can move beyond punitive cycles of blame and retaliation towards a more compassionate and collaborative approach to addressing conflicts and repairing harm.

Ultimately, the journey towards deconstructing enemies is

a profound and multifaceted endeavor that requires courage, humility, and a commitment to empathy-driven action. By embracing empathy, practicing perspective-taking, and engaging in authentic dialogue, we can transcend divisions, cultivate understanding, and forge meaningful connections across perceived divides. In doing so, we honor our shared humanity and collective potential to build a more compassionate and peaceful world for generations to come.

C. Techniques for Disrupting Enemy Constructs

1. Recognizing Intersecting Systems of Oppression: In the pursuit of disrupting enemy constructs, it is crucial to acknowledge the intersecting systems of oppression that shape individual experiences and perpetuate conflicts. By understanding how power dynamics, privilege, and discrimination intersect across various social identities such as race, gender, class, and sexuality, we can unravel the complexities of enmity and work towards dismantling the structural barriers that divide us. Cultivating awareness of these interconnected systems allows us to address root causes of conflict and promote intersectional approaches to healing and reconciliation.
2. Centering Marginalized Voices and Lived Experiences: Disrupting enemy constructs requires centering the voices and lived experiences of those most affected by conflict and oppression. By amplifying the narratives of marginalized communities, listening to their stories, and validating their truths, we can challenge dominant

narratives that perpetuate enmity and exclusion. By recognizing the inherent worth and dignity of all individuals, especially those at the margins of society, we can begin to deconstruct enemy constructs and promote a more inclusive and equitable world.

3. Building Coalitions and Solidarity Across Differences: In the pursuit of disrupting enemy constructs, it is essential to build coalitions and solidarity across diverse communities and perspectives. By forging alliances based on shared values, mutual respect, and a commitment to justice, we can transcend divisive boundaries and work towards common goals of peace and understanding. Embracing the power of collective action and intersectional solidarity enables us to amplify our impact and create lasting change in the face of entrenched enmity.

4. Engaging in Transformative Justice and Healing Practices: Disrupting enemy constructs involves engaging in transformative justice practices that prioritize healing, accountability, and reconciliation over punitive measures. By embracing restorative justice approaches that focus on repairing harm, fostering empathy, and promoting healing for all parties involved, we can break the cycles of violence and resentment that fuel enmity. Creating spaces for dialogue, reconciliation, and collective healing allows us to transform conflicts into opportunities for growth and connection.

5. Nurturing a Culture of Empathy and Compassion: Central to the process of disrupting enemy constructs

is nurturing a culture of empathy, compassion, and understanding. By cultivating practices of active listening, empathy, and conflict resolution, we can create environments that prioritize human connection and mutual respect. Encouraging acts of kindness, generosity, and forgiveness towards ourselves and others fosters a culture of compassion that can transcend enmity and promote genuine reconciliation.

In conclusion, the journey of disrupting enemy constructs is a multifaceted and profound undertaking that requires a commitment to challenging entrenched power dynamics, amplifying marginalized voices, building coalitions across differences, engaging in transformative justice, and nurturing a culture of empathy and compassion. By embracing these advanced strategies and practices, we can lay the foundation for a more just, equitable, and interconnected world where enmity gives way to understanding, solidarity, and peace.

* * *

Bibliography

Armour, Leslie. "Self Deconstruction and Possibility." Études Maritainiennes / Maritain Studies 10 (1994): 79–108. https://doi.org/10.5840/maritain1994107.

Delori, Mathias, and Vron Ware. "The Faces of Enmity

in International Relations. An Introduction." Critical Military Studies 5, no. 4 (September 25, 2019): 299–303. https://doi.org/10.1080/23337486.2019.1652460.

Ewelukwa, Uchechukwu. "Post-Colonialism, Gender, Customary Injustice: Widows in African Societies." Human Rights Quarterly 24, no. 2 (2002): 424–86. https://doi.org/10.1353/hrq.2002.0021.

Fawkner, H W. Deconstructing Macbeth : The Hyper-ontological View. Rutherford, N.J.: Fairleigh Dickinson University Press, 1990.

Feldman, Allen. "The Structuring Enemy and Archival War." PMLA/Publications of the Modern Language Association of America 124, no. 5 (October 2009): 1704–13. https://doi.org/10.1632/pmla.2009.124.5.1704.

Feldman A. The Structuring Enemy and Archival War. PMLA/Publications of the Modern Language Association of America. 2009;124(5):1704-1713. doi:10.1632/pmla.2009.124.5.1704

Fellman, Gordon. "Enemy, Concept and Identity Of." Elsevier EBooks, January 1, 2008, 681–90. https://doi.org/10.1016/b978-012373985-8.00057-x.

Gross, James J. "The Emerging Field of Emotion Regulation: An Integrative Review." Review of General Psychology 2, no. 3 (1998): 271–99. https://doi.org/10.1037/1089-2680.2.3.271.

Janzen, Christina. "The Social Construction of the 'Enemy' in a Post 911 Era," January 1, 2008. https://doi.org/10.20381/ruor-18785.

Maria Luisa Maniscalco. "Constructing/Deconstructing the Enemy: A Sociological Perspective," January 1, 2005.

McBride, Michael, and David Hewitt. "The Enemy You Can't See: An Investigation of the Disruption of Dark Networks." Journal of Economic Behavior and Organization 93 (September 1, 2013): 32–50. https://doi.org/10.1016/j.jebo.2013.07.004.

Mendes, Cristiano, and Karina Junqueira. "Drones, Warfare and the Deconstruction of the Enemy." Contexto Internacional 42, no. 2 (August 2020): 237–56. https://doi.org/10.1590/s0102-8529.2019420200002.

Olsen, Lance. "DECONSTRUCTING the ENEMY of COLOR: THE FANTASTIC in GRAVITY'S RAINBOW," January 1, 2016.

Prasad, Ajnesh. "The Organization of Ideological Discourse in Times of Unexpected Crisis: Explaining How COVID-19 Is Exploited by Populist Leaders." Leadership, May 12, 2020, 174271502092678. https://doi.org/10.1177/1742715020926783.

Riggs, Karen, Susan Tyler Eastman, and Timothy S Golobic. "Manufactured Conflict in the 1992 Olympics: The Discourse of Television and Politics1." Critical Studies in Mass Communication 10, no. 3 (September 1, 1993): 253–72. https://doi.org/10.1080/15295039309366867.

Ryan, Richard M. "Psychological Needs and the Facilitation of Integrative Processes." Journal of Personality 63, no. 3 (September 1995): 397–427.

Santos, Eugene, and Allesandro Negri. "Constructing Adversarial Models for Threat/Enemy Intent Prediction and Inferencing." Proceedings of SPIE, August 13, 2004. https://doi.org/10.1117/12.546771.

Stetsenko, Anna, and Igor Arievitch. "Constructing and Deconstructing the Self: Comparing Post-Vygotskian and Discourse-Based Versions of Social Constructivism." Mind, Culture, and Activity 4, no. 3 (July 1997): 159–72. https://doi.org/10.1207/s15327884mca0403_3.

Yost, John H., Michael J Strube, and James R. Bailey. "The Construction of the Self: An Evolutionary View." Current Psychology 11, no. 2 (June 1992): 110–21. https://doi.org/10.1007/bf02686833.

5

Achieving Control and Serenity

- Embracing Vulnerability and Uncertainty

In the quest for control and serenity, one must boldly embrace vulnerability and uncertainty. Although these concepts may initially trigger feelings of discomfort or fear, it is through acknowledging and accepting our vulnerabilities that we can truly thrive. Vulnerability is not a sign of weakness but rather a gateway to profound growth and resilience. By allowing ourselves to be vulnerable, we open the door to deep connections with others and foster a greater sense of authenticity within ourselves.

Moreover, uncertainty is an inevitable part of life that often triggers feelings of anxiety and unrest. However, by learning to sit with uncertainty and embrace the unknown, we can cultivate a sense of inner peace and adaptability. Instead of grasping for control in every situation, we can learn to trust in our own ability to navigate the unpredictable nature of life with grace and courage.

- Cultivating Inner Peace through Enemy Deconstruction

One of the most profound paths to achieving control and serenity is through the practice of deconstructing our perceptions of enemies. By recognizing that our concept of an enemy is often a construct influenced by our own biases and fears, we can begin to dismantle the barriers that separate us from others. Through empathy and understanding, we can break down the walls of hostility and cultivate a sense of compassion and connection with those we once saw as adversaries.

Engaging in enemy deconstruction is not about excusing harmful behavior or betraying our principles. Instead, it is a transformative process that allows us to see beyond the surface and recognize the shared humanity that binds us all. By seeking to understand the motivations and experiences of others, we can release ourselves from the burden of resentment and animosity, paving the way for inner peace and reconciliation.

- Practical Strategies for Maintaining Control and Serenity

To sustain control and serenity in the midst of life's challenges, it is essential to incorporate practical strategies into our daily routines. Mindfulness practices, such as meditation and breathing exercises, can help us stay grounded and centered in the present moment, allowing us to navigate stress and uncertainty with clarity and calmness. Setting boundaries and prioritizing self-care is also crucial in preserving our mental and emotional well-being, as it empowers us to honor our needs and protect our inner peace.

Furthermore, seeking support from trusted friends and loved ones can provide us with the strength and reassurance needed to weather difficult times. Engaging in activities that bring us joy and fulfillment nourishes the soul and replenishes our spirit, enhancing our overall sense of control and serenity. By integrating these strategies into our daily lives, we can cultivate a deep reservoir of resilience and inner peace that empowers us to face life's challenges with grace and fortitude.

A. Embracing Vulnerability and Uncertainty

In a world that often demands strength and certainty, embracing vulnerability and uncertainty can feel like a radical act. However, it is through this embrace that we can find true liberation and inner peace.

Vulnerability is often misunderstood as a sign of weakness, but in reality, it is a profound expression of courage and authenticity. When we allow ourselves to be vulnerable, we strip away the masks we wear and reveal our true selves to the world. This raw honesty not only deepens our connection with others but also strengthens our connection with ourselves. By embracing vulnerability, we acknowledge our imperfections and insecurities, paving the way for self-acceptance and self-compassion.

Moreover, vulnerability is the cornerstone of genuine intimacy and trust. When we are willing to let our guard down and expose our vulnerabilities, we create space for meaningful relationships to flourish. It is in these moments of openness and honesty that we forge deep connections based on empathy and understanding. By sharing our fears and struggles, we invite others to do the same, fostering a sense of mutual support and acceptance. Vulnerability, far from being a weakness, is a powerful catalyst for authentic human connection.

Similarly, uncertainty is a ubiquitous aspect of life that often triggers anxiety and discomfort. We naturally crave stability and control, but the truth is that uncertainty is an inherent part of the human experience. Embracing uncertainty involves surrendering the illusion of control and leaning into the ebb and flow of life.

Although uncertainty can be unsettling, it is also a fertile ground for growth and transformation. When we relinquish our need for predictability, we open ourselves up to a world of endless possibilities and opportunities. Embracing uncertainty cultivates a spirit of openness and curiosity, inviting us to embrace change and embrace the unknown with a sense of wonder and excitement. Instead of viewing uncertainty as a threat, we can see it as an invitation to welcome new experiences and challenges that enrich our lives.

By embracing vulnerability and uncertainty, we cultivate resilience and strength in the face of life's unpredictable nature. Rather than being paralyzed by fear and doubt, we learn to navigate the uncertainties of life with courage and grace. This acceptance allows us to move through life's challenges with a sense of flexibility and adaptability, embodying a spirit of resilience that empowers us to face the unknown with confidence and grace.

In surrendering to vulnerability and uncertainty, we invite a profound sense of freedom and empowerment into our lives. Embracing these essential aspects of our humanity enables us to transcend our fears and limitations, opening us up to a deeper connection with ourselves and others. Through vulnerability and uncertainty, we discover the true essence of our being and find strength in our ability to navigate the ever-changing landscape of life with grace and resilience.

B. Cultivating Inner Peace through Enemy Deconstruction

In the quest for inner peace, one of the most profound and transformative practices we can engage in is the process of deconstructing our perceived enemies. This practice delves deep into the core of our being, unraveling the intricate tapestry of beliefs, biases, and emotions that fuel our enmity towards others. By embarking on this journey of self-exploration and reflection, we not only liberate ourselves from the burden of hatred and resentment but also uncover a wellspring of compassion, forgiveness, and interconnectedness that lay dormant within us.

Enemy deconstruction is a multifaceted process that requires a willingness to confront the shadows of our psyche and the courage to face the uncomfortable truths that lie beneath the surface. It demands that we question the narratives we have constructed about our enemies and challenge the validity of our judgments. By peeling back the layers of conditioning and societal influences, we can begin to see our perceived enemies not as adversaries to be defeated but as fellow human beings on their own journey of struggle and suffering.

Empathy emerges as a guiding light in this process, illuminating the path towards understanding, connection, and reconciliation. Through the practice of empathetic listening and compassionate observation, we can cultivate a deeper sense of empathy towards our enemies, recognizing their joys, sorrows, fears, and aspirations as reflections of our own humanity. This shift in perspective creates a bridge of understanding that transcends the barriers of animosity and division, paving the way for healing and transformation.

Practical tools and techniques serve as invaluable allies in the journey of enemy deconstruction. Mindfulness practices, such as meditation, breathwork, and body scan exercises, can help us anchor ourselves in the present moment and cultivate a sense of inner calm and clarity. Journaling, self-inquiry, and therapeutic interventions offer us space for self-reflection and introspection, allowing us to excavate the deep-seated roots of our hostility and transform them into seeds of compassion and growth.

As we continue to delve deeper into the realm of enemy deconstruction, we may encounter resistance, discomfort, and uncertainty. This is a natural part of the process, signaling the breaking down of old patterns and belief systems that no longer serve our highest good. By embracing this discomfort with courage and openness, we can navigate through the turbulent waters of inner conflict and emerge on the shores of inner peace and reconciliation.

In essence, cultivating inner peace through enemy deconstruction is a sacred journey of self-discovery, healing, and transformation. It invites us to confront the shadows of our own psyche, transcend the limitations of duality and separation, and embrace the interconnectedness and unity that underlies all of existence. In this process, we discover that our perceived enemies are but reflections of ourselves, mirrors that reflect back to us the parts of ourselves that are in need of healing and integration. Through the alchemy of compassion, forgiveness, and self-awareness, we can transcend the shackles of hatred and division and embrace a more profound sense of harmony, wholeness, and peace within ourselves and the world around us.

Developing a daily practice of self-reflection and introspection can further deepen our understanding of the roots of our enmity and help us cultivate a greater sense of self-awareness and empathy. By setting aside dedicated time each day to journal, meditate, or engage in other mindfulness activities, we can create a space for inner exploration and growth, allowing us to uncover hidden beliefs, emotions, and narratives that shape our perceptions of others.

Moreover, seeking out opportunities for dialogue and communication with those we perceive as enemies can also facilitate the process of enemy deconstruction. Engaging in open, honest, and compassionate conversations with individuals whose perspectives differ from our own can challenge our assumptions, broaden our horizons, and foster a deeper sense of empathy and understanding. By approaching these interactions with a mindset of curiosity, openness, and respect, we can create a space for authentic connection and mutual learning that transcends the boundaries of discord and animosity.

In our journey towards inner peace through enemy deconstruction, it is essential to embrace the power of forgiveness as a catalyst for healing and transformation. Forgiveness does not mean condoning or excusing the harmful actions of others; rather, it is a radical act of self-love and liberation that releases us from the burden of resentment and allows us to reclaim our inner sovereignty. By extending forgiveness towards ourselves and others, we free ourselves from the chains of the past and open our hearts to the possibility of renewal, reconciliation, and harmony.

As we continue to navigate the complex terrain of inner conflict and external strife, let us remember that the path of enemy deconstruction is not a linear journey but a spiraling evolution towards greater wholeness and unity. It invites us to embrace the paradoxes of our humanity, acknowledging the interplay of light and shadow, love and fear, unity and division within ourselves and the world around us. Through this profound process of self-discovery and transformation, we can transcend the illusion of separation and cultivate a more profound sense of inner peace, compassion, and connection that reverberates throughout the tapestry of existence.

C. Practical Strategies for Maintaining Control and Serenity

Incorporating practical strategies for maintaining control and serenity in our lives is essential for navigating the ebbs and flows of daily challenges and uncertainties. In this extended version of the chapter, we will delve even deeper into specific techniques and practices that can help cultivate a sense of empowerment and peace in the face of life's complexities.

One powerful strategy for maintaining control and serenity is the practice of mindfulness. This involves cultivating a deep sense of presence and awareness in the present moment, which can help us tap into our inner wisdom and respond to situations from a place of clarity and calm. Through mindfulness practices such as meditation, deep breathing exercises, and body scans, we can train our minds to focus on the present moment rather than getting swept away by worries about the future or regrets about the past.

Another important aspect of maintaining control and serenity is developing emotional intelligence. This involves recognizing and understanding our own emotions and those of others, and learning how to respond to them in healthy and constructive ways. By honing our emotional intelligence skills, we can better regulate our emotions, communicate effectively with others, and navigate through difficult situations with grace and empathy.

Cultivating a positive mindset is also crucial for maintaining control and serenity in our lives. By practicing gratitude, focusing on the bright side of situations, and nurturing self-compassion, we can shift our perspective towards one that is more optimistic and resilient. A positive mindset can help us weather the storms of life with greater ease, bounce back from setbacks more quickly, and maintain a sense of hope and possibility even in challenging times.

Setting boundaries and prioritizing self-care are foundational practices for maintaining control and serenity. By establishing clear boundaries around our time, energy, and relationships, we can protect our well-being and ensure that we are not overextending ourselves. Prioritizing self-care activities such as exercise, healthy eating, rest, and relaxation can help us recharge and rejuvenate our bodies and minds, enabling us to face life's demands with vitality and resilience.

Lastly, practicing acceptance and letting go of the need for control can be a profound way to maintain serenity in our lives. Acceptance does not mean resignation or passivity; rather, it is about acknowledging reality as it is and making peace with it. By surrendering our attachment to outcomes and embracing the flow of life, we can cultivate a deep sense of peace and freedom within ourselves.

By integrating these deep and transformative practices into our daily lives, we can enhance our ability to maintain control and serenity in the face of life's challenges and uncertainties. Embracing mindfulness, emotional intelligence, a positive mindset, boundaries, self-care, and acceptance can empower us to navigate through life with grace, resilience, and inner peace.

* * *

Bibliography

Akre, Rajat. LIFE RECKONER,12 PRINCIPLES for WELLBEING. Booksclinic Publishing, 2023.

Arora, Saurabh, Barbara Van Dyck, Divya Sharma, and Andy Stirling. "Control, Care, and Conviviality in the Politics of Technology for Sustainability." Sustainability: Science, Practice and Policy 16, no. 1 (October 22, 2020): 247–62. https://doi.org/10.1080/15487733.2020.1816687.

Berkes, Fikret. "Understanding Uncertainty and Reducing Vulnerability: Lessons from Resilience Thinking." Natural Hazards 41, no. 2 (January 16, 2007): 283–95. https://doi.org/10.1007/s11069-006-9036-7.

Bodenhausen, Galen V., Geoffrey P. Kramer, and Karin Süsser. "Happiness and Stereotypic Thinking in Social Judgment." Journal of Personality and Social Psychology 66, no. 4 (1994): 621–32. https://doi.org/10.1037/0022-3514.66.4.621.

Brown, Brené. Daring Greatly. Penguin UK, 2013.

Camilla Funck Ellehave, Erin Wilson Burns, and Dave Ulrich. "Embracing and Harnessing Uncertainty." IGI Global EBooks, January 1, 2021, 21–40. https://doi.org/10.4018/978-1-7998-7016-6.ch002.

Desilet, Gregory, and Edward C. Appel. "Choosing a Rhetoric of the Enemy: Kenneth Burke's Comic Frame, Warrantable Outrage, and the Problem of Scapegoating."

Rhetoric Society Quarterly 41, no. 4 (July 2011): 340–62. https://doi.org/10.1080/02773945.2011.596177.

"Embracing Uncertainty." Routledge EBooks, June 26, 2015, 189–200. https://doi.org/10.4324/9781315689425-8.

Fenyk, Cassandra. Embracing Imperfections: Unleashing Our Perfect Selves. Fenyk Enterprises LLC, 2023.

Floody, Dale R. "Serenity and Inner Peace: Positive Perspectives." Peace Psychology Book Series, November 6, 2013, 107–33. https://doi.org/10.1007/978-1-4614-9366-2_5.

Fredrickson, Barbara L. "What Good Are Positive Emotions?" Review of General Psychology 2, no. 3 (1998): 300–319. https://doi.org/10.1037/1089-2680.2.3.300.

Gehart, Diane R., and Eric E. McCollum. "Engaging Suffering: Towards a Mindful Re-Visioning of Family Therapy Practice." Journal of Marital and Family Therapy 33, no. 2 (April 2007): 214–26. https://doi.org/10.1111/j.1752-0606.2007.00017.x.

Giri, Ananta Kumar. "Rethinking Human Well-Being: A Dialogue with Amartya Sen." Journal of International Development 12, no. 7 (2000): 1003–18. https://doi.org/10.1002/1099-1328(200010)12:7%3C1003::aid-jid698%3E3.0.co;2-u.

Gur-Ze'ev, Ilan. "PHILOSOPHY of PEACE EDUCATION in a POSTMODERN ERA." Educational Theory 51, no. 3 (September 2001): 315–36. https://doi.org/10.1111/j.1741-5446.2001.00315.x.

Seligman, Martin E. P., and Mihaly Csikszentmihalyi. "Positive Psychology: An Introduction." American Psychologist 55, no. 1 (January 2000): 5–14. https://doi.org/10.1037/0003-066x.55.1.5.

Shapiro, Deane H. "Reflections on the Role of Control in Meditation." Oxford University Press EBooks, December 15, 2020. https://doi.org/10.1093/oxfordhb/9780198808640.013.49.

Singh, Anila. Redefining Normal! Embracing and Celebrating Your Individuality. Writers Corner Publication, 2024.

Sinko, Laura, Courtney Julia Burns, Sharon O'Halloran, and Denise Saint Arnault. "Trauma Recovery Is Cultural: Understanding Shared and Different Healing Themes in Irish and American Survivors of Gender-Based Violence." Journal of Interpersonal Violence, February 19, 2019, 088626051982928. https://doi.org/10.1177/0886260519829284.

Soni, Harshwardhan. Eternal Thirst the Quest for Enlightenment. Harsh Wardhan Soni, 2024.

Stein, Ruth. "Fundamentalism, Father and Son, and Vertical Desire." The Psychoanalytic Review 93, no. 2 (April 2006): 201–30. https://doi.org/10.1521/prev.2006.93.2.201.

Sword-Daniels, Victoria, Christine Eriksen, Emma E. Hudson-Doyle, Ryan Alaniz, Carolina Adler, Todd Schenk, and Suzanne Vallance. "Embodied Uncertainty: Living with Complexity and Natural Hazards." Journal of Risk Research 21, no. 3 (July 8, 2016): 290–307. https://doi.org/10.1080/13669877.2016.1200659.

Trenton, Nick. KEEP CALM. PKCS Media, 2024.

Wong, David B. "The Meaning of Detachment in Daoism, Buddhism, and Stoicism." Dao 5, no. 2 (June 2006): 207–19. https://doi.org/10.1007/bf02868031.

6

Application in Daily Life

A. Relationships: Deconstructing Personal Enemies

In our daily lives, we encounter various individuals who may trigger feelings of animosity or enmity within us. These personal enemies can range from family members to colleagues to acquaintances. By applying the principles of self-awareness and enemy deconstruction, we can navigate these relationships with a sense of understanding and compassion.

Instead of reacting impulsively to perceived slights or disagreements, we can pause and reflect on the underlying factors that contribute to our negative feelings towards these individuals. Through self-reflection, we may uncover deep-seated insecurities or past traumas that color our perception of others as enemies.

Empathy and perspective-taking play a crucial role in deconstructing personal enemies. By putting ourselves in the shoes of the other person, we can gain a better understanding of their motivations, fears, and vulnerabilities. This shift in perspective can humanize the other person and make it easier for us to let go of animosity and resentment.

Practical strategies for deconstructing personal enemies include engaging in open and honest communication, setting boundaries, and practicing forgiveness. By fostering constructive dialogue and mutual respect, we can cultivate healthier and more fulfilling relationships with those we once viewed as enemies.

B. Societal and Political Contexts: Deconstructing Collective Enemies

Beyond individual relationships, society and politics are rife with the construction of collective enemies. Whether it be political opponents, rival nations, or marginalized groups, the notion of "us versus them" pervades our social fabric and colors our interactions with others.

Deconstructing collective enemies requires a critical examination of the narratives and ideologies that perpetuate division and animosity. By challenging stereotypical beliefs and seeking out diverse perspectives, we can begin to unravel the fabric of collective enmity.

Case studies and real-life examples offer valuable insights into the dynamics of collective enemy construction. By studying historical and contemporary conflicts, we can uncover the root causes of societal division and explore alternative paths towards reconciliation and unity.

Ultimately, the process of deconstructing collective enemies is a collective endeavor that requires empathy, dialogue, and a commitment to social justice. By working together to challenge oppressive systems and dismantle harmful narratives, we can create a more inclusive and equitable society for all.

A. Relationships: Deconstructing Personal Enemies

Forgiveness is a profound act that transcends the boundaries of individual relationships and extends to the collective consciousness of humanity. It is a transformative process that holds the power to heal not only personal wounds but also societal rifts and historical injustices. By deconstructing personal enemies, we unravel the intricate web of interconnections that bind us together as human beings, sharing a common journey of growth and evolution.

As we delve deeper into the complexities of forgiveness, we recognize that it is not a one-time event but an ongoing practice that requires patience, humility, and perseverance. It involves a deep exploration of our own vulnerabilities, fears, and insecurities, as well as an acknowledgment of the inherent humanity within those we perceive as enemies. By embracing our shared humanity, we cultivate empathy and compassion, bridging the divide between self and other.

In the process of deconstructing personal enemies, we confront the shadows within ourselves and society, acknowledging the systemic injustices and power imbalances that perpetuate cycles of conflict and harm. By shining a light on these shadows, we create space for healing, reconciliation, and transformation. Through courageous conversations, restorative justice practices, and community engagement, we can work towards dismantling the walls of animosity and building bridges of understanding and cooperation.

Furthermore, as we navigate the terrain of personal enemies, we must also confront the role of forgiveness in the broader context of social change and collective healing. By engaging in truth-telling, accountability, and reparative actions, we sow the seeds of transformation and create a ripple effect of healing that extends far beyond individual relationships. Forgiveness becomes a revolutionary act that disrupts cycles of violence and oppression, paving the way for a more just, compassionate, and interconnected world.

In essence, the process of deconstructing personal enemies is a profound journey of self-discovery, reconciliation, and growth that transcends the boundaries of individual conflicts and embraces the universal principles of forgiveness and unity. By embracing the challenges and complexities of forgiveness with an open heart and a courageous spirit, we can unleash the transformative power of healing and create a more peaceful and harmonious world for all.

B. Societal and Political Contexts: Deconstructing Collective Enemies

In exploring the intricacies of how collective enemies are constructed within societal and political contexts, we unearth a profound understanding of the complex interplay between identity, power dynamics, and historical narratives. The phenomenon of collective enemy construction is not a mere coincidence but rather a deliberate strategy employed by leaders and institutions to maintain control, foster unity, and justify their actions through the manipulation of perceptions and emotions.

At the heart of constructing collective enemies lies the fundamental human impulse to define oneself in opposition to others. This age-old practice is deeply rooted in the evolutionary psychology of ingroup favoritism and outgroup hostility, where individuals naturally gravitate towards those who they perceive as similar and differentiate themselves from those who are perceived as different. Societal and political leaders have long capitalized on this innate tendency to stoke fears, prejudice, and animosity towards certain groups, thereby solidifying their own authority and influence.

Moreover, the construction of collective enemies is intricately linked to the power dynamics within society. By creating a common enemy to rally against, leaders can galvanize support, deflect attention from internal issues or failures, and justify the implementation of discriminatory measures or policies. This tactic not only serves to maintain a sense of control and hierarchy but also reinforces existing power structures by delineating who belongs and who is excluded from the collective identity.

The manipulation of narratives and historical memory also plays a crucial role in collective enemy construction. By distorting facts, emphasizing certain events, and omitting others, leaders can shape public perceptions of the enemy as a threat to the very fabric of society. This selective framing of history serves to solidify the us-versus-them mentality, perpetuate intergenerational animosities, and fuel a sense of collective victimhood that justifies hostile actions or rhetoric towards the perceived enemy.

Furthermore, the media and propaganda machinery act as powerful tools in amplifying and sustaining collective enemy constructs. Through the dissemination of sensationalized stories, biased portrayals, and inflammatory rhetoric, media outlets can manipulate public opinion, reinforce stereotypes, and breed a culture of fear and mistrust towards certain groups. This weaponization of information not only deepens societal divisions but also hampers efforts towards reconciliation, dialogue, and understanding across different segments of society.

To dismantle the harmful effects of collective enemy constructs, it is imperative to foster critical thinking, empathy, and solidarity among individuals and communities. By proactively challenging prejudices, engaging in open dialogue with diverse perspectives, and cultivating a culture of inclusivity and respect, we can begin to break down the barriers that sustain collective enemies. Building bridges of understanding and empathy across societal divides is essential in creating a more cohesive, compassionate, and just society where collective enemies hold no sway.

In conclusion, the deconstruction of collective enemies necessitates a comprehensive approach that addresses the deep-seated societal, political, and psychological factors at play. By illuminating the mechanisms of collective enemy construction, promoting empathy and dialogue, and advocating for a more nuanced understanding of identity and power dynamics, we can pave the way towards a world free from the damaging influences of collective enemies and towards a future rooted in unity, cooperation, and mutual respect.

C. Case Studies and Real-Life Examples

As we continue to explore the profound impact of understanding the enemy and self-awareness in real-life contexts, it becomes evident that these principles hold the key to transforming relationships and resolving conflicts on a deeper level. By delving into additional case studies and scenarios, we gain further insights into the complexities of human nature and the power of empathy in overcoming barriers to connection and understanding.

One compelling case study that exemplifies the transformative potential of self-awareness and the deconstruction of enemy constructs is the story of a nation torn apart by political polarization and historical grievances. In this scenario, deep-rooted animosities and narratives of victimhood had fueled decades of conflict, leading to a cycle of violence and mistrust. However, through a series of truth and reconciliation initiatives that encouraged individuals to confront their own biases and perceptions, a shift began to occur.

By creating spaces for open dialogue, acknowledging past injustices, and fostering empathy for the experiences of others, individuals from opposing factions were able to humanize the "enemy" and recognize the shared humanity that transcended their differences. This led to a gradual process of healing and reconciliation, paving the way for a more sustainable peace based on mutual understanding and respect.

Moreover, the application of self-awareness and empathy in personal relationships and everyday interactions can have a profound ripple effect, influencing positive change on a micro level that reverberates outward. By cultivating a greater awareness of our own emotions, triggers, and biases, we not only enhance our ability to navigate conflicts constructively but also create opportunities for deeper connections and authentic communication with others.

In the realm of societal issues, the power of understanding the enemy and self-awareness is particularly salient when addressing systemic injustices and entrenched divisions. By acknowledging the ways in which historical narratives and structural inequalities have shaped our perceptions of "others," we can begin to challenge ingrained prejudices and work towards building a more inclusive and equitable society.

Through continued reflection, dialogue, and action grounded in empathy and self-awareness, we have the potential to break down barriers, bridge divides, and forge a path towards a more harmonious and interconnected world. The journey towards understanding the enemy and embracing our own complexity is not always easy, but it is undoubtedly transformative, offering the promise of a brighter future built on compassion, recognition, and genuine human connection.

* * *

Bibliography

A J P Thomson. Deconstruction and Democracy : Derrida's Politics of Friendship. London ; New York: Continuum, 2007.

Berntzen, Lars Erik, and Sveinung Sandberg. "The Collective Nature of Lone Wolf Terrorism: Anders Behring Breivik and the Anti-Islamic Social Movement." Terrorism and Political Violence 26, no. 5 (February 5, 2014): 759–79. https://doi.org/10.1080/09546553.2013.767245.

Bond, Mel. Understanding Your Worst Enemy, 1992.

Cerulo, Karen A. "Identity Construction: New Issues, New Directions." Annual Review of Sociology 23, no. 1 (1997): 385–409. https://doi.org/10.1146/annurev.soc.23.1.385.

Chang, Briankle G. Deconstructing Communication. U of Minnesota Press, 1996.

Delori, Mathias, and Vron Ware. "The Faces of Enmity in International Relations. An Introduction." Critical Military Studies 5, no. 4 (September 25, 2019): 299–303. https://doi.org/10.1080/23337486.2019.1652460.

Fraser, Heather. "Doing Narrative Research." Qualitative Social Work: Research and Practice 3, no. 2 (June 2004): 179–201. https://doi.org/10.1177/1473325004043383.

GODSWORD GODSWILL ONU. UNDERSTANDING the STRATEGIES of YOUR ENEMY. Lulu.com, n.d.

Habeck, Mary R. Knowing the Enemy : Jihadist Ideology

and the War on Terror. New Haven, Conn.: Yale University Press, 2007.

Halifax, Joan. "The Precious Necessity of Compassion." Journal of Pain and Symptom Management 41, no. 1 (January 2011): 146–53. https://doi.org/10.1016/j.jpainsymman.2010.08.010.

Juengel, Scott J. "William Blake's Enemies." SEL Studies in English Literature 1500-1900 58, no. 3 (2018): 703–29. https://doi.org/10.1353/sel.2018.0028.

Latour, Bruno. "Why Has Critique Run out of Steam? From Matters of Fact to Matters of Concern." Critical Inquiry 30, no. 2 (January 2022): 225–48. https://doi.org/10.1086/421123.

Merskin, Debra. "Making Enemies in George W. Bush's Post-9/11 Speeches." Peace Review 17, no. 4 (October 2005): 373–81. https://doi.org/10.1080/10402650500374637.

Murer, Jeffrey Stevenson. "Constructing the Enemy-Other: Anxiety, Trauma and Mourning in the Narratives of Political Conflict." Psychoanalysis, Culture & Society 14, no. 2 (June 24, 2009): 109–30. https://doi.org/10.1057/pcs.2008.33.

Newman, David, and Anssi Paasi. "Fences and Neighbours in the Postmodern World: Boundary Narratives in Political Geography." Progress in Human Geography 22, no. 2 (April 1998): 186–207. https://doi.org/10.1191/030913298666039113.

Okocha, Desmond Onyemechi, Muhammad Yousaf, and Onobe, Melchizedec J. Handbook of Research on Deconstructing Culture and Communication in the Global South. IGI Global, 2023.

Polletta, Francesca, and James M. Jasper. "Collective Identity and Social Movements." Annual Review of Sociology 27, no. 1 (August 2001): 283–305. https://doi.org/10.1146/annurev.soc.27.1.283.

Prozorov, Sergei. "Liberal Enmity: The Figure of the Foe in the Political Ontology of Liberalism." Millennium: Journal of International Studies 35, no. 1 (December 2006): 75–99. https://doi.org/10.1177/03058298060350010801.

Senatore, Mauro. Performatives after Deconstruction. New York: Bloomsbury Publishing Plc, 2013.

Shore, Zachary. A Sense of the Enemy : The High-Stakes History of Reading Your Rival's Mind. Oxford: Oxford University Press, 2014.

Sunzi, and Carl Von Clausewitz. The Book of War. New York: Modern Library, 2000.

7

The Art of Serenity

As individuals delve deeper into the art of serenity, they uncover hidden reservoirs of strength and resilience within themselves. This journey of self-discovery is not merely about finding temporary moments of calm, but about forging a profound sense of inner peace that withstands the trials and tribulations of life. It is a transformative process that requires dedication, patience, and a willingness to confront the shadows lurking within.

One of the key pillars of the art of serenity is the cultivation of self-awareness. This introspective practice involves turning inward and examining the intricate tapestry of one's thoughts, emotions, and beliefs. By shining a light on the inner landscape, individuals can untangle the knots of confusion and conflict, gaining clarity and insight into their true nature.

Self-awareness also entails acknowledging and accepting the full spectrum of one's emotions, including pain, fear, and sadness. By embracing these difficult emotions with

DECONSTRUCTING THE ENEMY

compassion and gentleness, individuals can transmute them into sources of wisdom and growth. This process of emotional alchemy enables one to deepen their connection to themselves and others, fostering empathy and understanding in the face of adversity.

Another crucial aspect of the art of serenity is the practice of self-care and self-compassion. Taking time to nurture and nourish oneself is essential for building a strong foundation of inner peace. This includes engaging in activities that bring joy and fulfillment, setting boundaries to protect one's energy, and treating oneself with kindness and grace.

Mindfulness, a cornerstone of the art of serenity, invites individuals to cultivate a deep sense of presence and engagement with the world around them. By fully immersing themselves in the sights, sounds, and sensations of the present moment, individuals can anchor themselves in the here and now, letting go of distractions and worries. Mindfulness also fosters a sense of interconnectedness with all beings, cultivating a spirit of compassion and unity.

As individuals deepen their practice of serenity, they begin to embody a sense of equanimity and balance that radiates outwards, influencing and inspiring those around them. This ripple effect of peace and serenity creates a ripple effect that can transform relationships, communities, and even the world at large. In a world rife with discord and division, the art of serenity stands as a beacon of hope and healing, offering a path to unity and understanding.

Ultimately, the art of serenity is a lifelong journey, a continuous exploration of the depths of the human soul and the boundless potential for growth and transformation. By embracing this path with courage and humility, individuals can unlock the door to inner peace and spiritual fulfillment, walking the path of serenity with grace and gratitude.

A. Finding Calm Amidst Chaos

In the intricate tapestry of life, the quest for calm amidst chaos is a profound journey that calls upon us to delve deep into the innermost recesses of our being. Amidst the cacophony of the world, where distractions clamor for our attention and stressors threaten to overwhelm our senses, finding moments of tranquility and equipoise becomes a sacred art to be mastered.

At the core of this search for serenity lies the practice of mindfulness – the art of being fully present in the moment without judgment or attachment to the past or future. Through mindful awareness, we can learn to observe the swirling currents of thoughts and emotions within us without being swept away by their turbulent tides. This mindful presence allows us to anchor ourselves in the stillness at the heart of our being, where a profound sense of peace and clarity resides.

Moreover, the cultivation of inner stillness amidst external chaos requires a commitment to self-care practices that nourish the body, mind, and spirit. Engaging in activities that promote physical well-being, such as regular exercise, healthy eating, and adequate rest, lays a solid foundation for emotional resilience and mental clarity. Additionally, carving out sacred moments of solitude and reflection in our daily lives provides a sanctuary for introspection and renewal, allowing us to recharge and replenish our inner resources.

Furthermore, the power of acceptance emerges as a transformative force in our quest for calm amidst chaos. By embracing the inherent impermanence and unpredictability of life, we can release the grip of resistance and open ourselves to the flow of existence with grace and equanimity. Acceptance does not signify passive resignation but rather a courageous acknowledgment of reality, empowering us to respond to challenges with wisdom and discernment.

In our pursuit of tranquility amidst turmoil, we are reminded of the significance of fostering meaningful connections with others. Building a support network of compassionate souls who can provide solace, guidance, and companionship during turbulent times is essential for maintaining emotional well-being and fortitude. Sharing our vulnerabilities and joys with trusted confidants can uplift our spirits and remind us of the interconnectedness that binds us all.

In essence, the path to finding calm amidst chaos is a sacred pilgrimage of self-discovery and growth, guided by the luminous beacon of inner peace that shines brightly within each of us. By embracing mindfulness, self-care, acceptance, and connection, we can navigate the turbulent waters of life with grace, resilience, and a deep-rooted sense of tranquility that transcends external circumstances.

B. Navigating Turbulent Waters with Grace

In times of adversity and turmoil, it is crucial to maintain a sense of composure and grace. This chapter delves into the strategies and mindset needed to navigate challenging circumstances with poise and resilience.

When faced with turbulent waters, it is important to first acknowledge and accept the situation at hand. Avoidance or denial will only prolong the inevitable and hinder your ability to address the challenges effectively. Embracing the reality of the situation is the first step towards finding a way through it.

Next, cultivate a sense of inward calm and strength. This can be achieved through practices such as mindfulness, meditation, and self-reflection. By grounding yourself in the present moment and connecting with your inner reserves of strength, you can better weather the storm and maintain a sense of stability amidst chaos.

Communication and collaboration are key components of navigating turbulent waters. Seek support from loved ones, mentors, or professionals who can offer guidance and perspective. By engaging with others and sharing your experiences, you can gain valuable insights and support that can help you navigate challenges with grace.

Furthermore, it is essential to practice self-care during turbulent times. Engage in activities that bring you joy and relaxation, whether it be spending time in nature, exercising, or pursuing creative outlets. Taking care of your physical and emotional well-being will provide you with the fortitude needed to face challenges head-on.

Maintaining a sense of perspective and resilience is crucial.

Remember that setbacks are not a reflection of your worth or abilities but rather opportunities for growth and learning. Embrace the journey of navigating turbulent waters as a path towards self-discovery and personal development.

In addition to inner strength, consider the power of adaptability. Being able to adjust and pivot when faced with unexpected obstacles or changes in direction is a valuable skill. Embrace flexibility and willingness to explore new approaches as you navigate through challenging times.

Moreover, cultivating emotional intelligence is paramount in navigating turbulent waters with grace. Understanding your own emotions and reactions, as well as being attuned to the emotions of others, can help you navigate difficult situations with empathy and understanding. By developing this awareness, you can respond thoughtfully and compassionately in the face of adversity.

In conclusion, navigating turbulent waters with grace requires a combination of acceptance, inner strength, communication, self-care, adaptability, resilience, and emotional intelligence. By embodying these qualities and approaches, you can navigate challenges with poise, resilience, and ultimately emerge stronger and wiser.

C. Creating Your Inner Sanctuary

In the midst of chaos and uncertainty, it is essential to create a sanctuary within ourselves. This inner refuge serves as a source of strength, calm, and stability in the face of adversity. By cultivating this sanctuary, we can find peace and tranquility even in the most turbulent times.

Our inner sanctuary is a sacred space that we can access anytime, anywhere. It is a place of solace and serenity, where we can retreat to recharge and rejuvenate our spirits. In this space, we are free from external pressures and distractions, allowing us to connect deeply with ourselves and find solace in our inner world.

Creating and nurturing our inner sanctuary requires intention and dedication. We must set aside time each day to cultivate this space, whether through meditation, mindfulness practices, or simply engaging in activities that bring us joy and peace. By consistently tending to our inner sanctuary, we strengthen its presence within us, making it a reliable source of comfort and support.

Within our inner sanctuary, we can release all worries and fears, allowing ourselves to be fully present in the moment. This space is a place of unconditional acceptance, where we can embrace our true selves without judgment or criticism. Here, we can find refuge from the chaos of the external world and connect with our inner wisdom and intuition.

As we deepen our relationship with our inner sanctuary, we develop a sense of inner peace and resilience. We learn to trust in ourselves and our innate ability to navigate life's challenges with grace and courage. This sanctuary becomes a beacon of light in the darkness, guiding us through difficult times and reminding us of our inner strength and power.

In times of turmoil and uncertainty, our inner sanctuary becomes a sanctuary of hope and inspiration. It is a place where we can find clarity and perspective, reconnecting with our deepest values and beliefs. By cultivating this inner refuge, we can weather any storm with grace and resilience, emerging stronger and more grounded than before.

Our inner sanctuary is not a stagnant space but a dynamic and evolving entity that grows and transforms with us. As we journey through life's ups and downs, our inner sanctuary adapts to our changing needs, providing us with the guidance and support we need at each stage of our journey. It is a mirror of our innermost selves, reflecting our deepest desires, fears, and aspirations back to us with compassion and understanding.

In the depths of our inner sanctuary, we find a profound sense of connection – to ourselves, to others, and to the universe at large. It is here that we discover the interconnectedness of all beings and the inherent wisdom that lies within each of us. This interconnectedness serves as a reminder of our shared humanity and the power of compassion and empathy to heal and transform.

In cultivating our inner sanctuary, we embark on a journey of self-discovery and self-compassion. We learn to embrace all aspects of ourselves – the light and the shadow, the joy and the sorrow – with acceptance and grace. Through this process, we come to realize that our inner sanctuary is not separate from the world around us but an integral part of it, infused with the same energy and essence that permeates all of creation.

As we continue to nurture and cultivate our inner sanctuary, we become beacons of light and love in the world, radiating our inner peace and serenity outward to those around us. Our inner sanctuary becomes a source of inspiration and empowerment for others, inviting them to embark on their own journey of self-discovery and inner transformation.

In the quiet depths of our inner sanctuary, we find solace, strength, and wisdom. It is a place of infinite potential and possibility, where we can tap into the wellspring of creativity, intuition, and insight that resides within us. By honoring and nurturing our inner sanctuary, we align ourselves with the deepest truths of our being and open ourselves to a life of purpose, fulfillment, and joy.

* * *

Bibliography

Adell, Emeli, Andras Varhelyi, and Lena Nilsson. "The Definition of Acceptance and Acceptability." CRC Press EBooks, September 3, 2018, 11–22. https://doi.org/10.1201/9781315578132-2.

Bennett, Richard, and Joseph E Oliver. "Acceptance." Routledge EBooks, March 27, 2019, 72–73. https://doi.org/10.4324/9781351056144-31.

———. "Acceptance Techniques." Routledge EBooks, March 27, 2019, 129–30. https://doi.org/10.4324/9781351056144-54.

Breines, Juliana, Aubrey Toole, Clarissa Tu, and Serena Chen. "Self-Compassion, Body Image, and Self-Reported Disordered Eating." Self and Identity 13, no. 4 (October 4, 2013): 432–48. https://doi.org/10.1080/15298868.2013.838992.

CARANFA, ANGELO. "Lessons of Solitude: The Awakening of Aesthetic Sensibility." Journal of Philosophy of Education 41, no. 1 (February 2007): 113–27. https://doi.org/10.1111/j.1467-9752.2007.00539.x.

Duckworth, Angela. "Cultivating Confidence." Character Lab Tips, December 2020. https://doi.org/10.53776/tips-cultivating-confidence.

———. "The Power of Praise: Positive Reinforcement Can Lead to Positive Outcomes." Character Lab Tip, March 27, 2022. https://doi.org/10.53776/power-of-praise.

González, Segundo, Ana Pilar González-Rodríguez, Alejandro López-Soto, Leticia Huergo-Zapico, Carlos López-Larrea, and B Suárez-Álvarez. "Conceptual Aspects of Self and Nonself Discrimination." Self/Nonself 2, no. 1 (January 2011): 19–25. https://doi.org/10.4161/self.2.1.15094.

Hansard, Christopher. The Tibetan Art of Serenity. Hachette UK, 2011.

Karasu, T. Byram. The Art of Serenity : The Path to a Joyful Life in the Best and Worst of Times. New York: Simon & Schuster, 2014.

Tang, Amy H. "Are You My Friends or Are You My Enemies?" Self/Nonself 2, no. 3 (June 2011): 142–46. https://doi.org/10.4161/self.20137.

Terry, Meredith L., and Mark R. Leary. "Self-Compassion, Self-Regulation, and Health." Self and Identity 10, no. 3 (July 2011): 352–62. https://doi.org/10.1080/15298868.2011.558404.

Wilkinson, Dee. "Re-Assessing Your Beliefs." Routledge EBooks, September 3, 2021, 29–34. https://doi.org/10.4324/9781003172734-5.

Xingxiu, and Thomas F Cleary. Book of Serenity : One Hundred Zen Dialogues. Boston, Mass.: Shambhala, 2005.

Yang, Xiaoyan. "The Passion behind Serenity." Asian Social Science 5, no. 1 (February 9, 2009). https://doi.org/10.5539/ass.v5n1p119.

8

The Mastery of Self-Awareness

A. Honing the Sword of Introspection

In the pursuit of self-awareness and personal growth, introspection serves as a powerful tool for exploring the depths of your inner being. By honing the sword of introspection, you can cut through the layers of conditioning, biases, and limiting beliefs that obscure your true self.

Begin by creating space for self-reflection in your daily life. Set aside dedicated time to sit in quiet contemplation, away from distractions and external influences. This practice allows you to delve into your thoughts, emotions, and actions with a sense of curiosity and openness.

As you engage in introspection, be willing to confront the uncomfortable truths that may arise. Acknowledge your fears, insecurities, and past traumas without judgment or self-criticism. This process of acceptance and self-love is essential for deepening your understanding of who you truly are.

The process of introspection is akin to peeling back the layers of an onion, revealing deeper truths and insights into your psyche. As you continue to wield the sword of introspection, you may uncover unconscious patterns of behavior, unresolved emotions, and unhealed wounds that have been lurking beneath the surface. By shining the light of awareness on these hidden aspects of yourself, you can begin the process of healing and transformation.

B. Guardian of Your Thoughts: The Power of Mindfulness

Mindfulness is another essential practice in the mastery of self-awareness. By staying present in the moment and observing your thoughts without attachment, you can cultivate a greater sense of clarity and insight into your inner world.

Practice mindfulness in your daily activities, whether it be during routine tasks, interactions with others, or moments of solitude. Bring awareness to your thoughts, emotions, and physical sensations without reacting impulsively or getting caught up in automatic patterns of behavior.

Through the practice of mindfulness, you can develop a greater sense of control over your mind and emotions. By observing your thoughts with detachment, you can choose how to respond to challenging situations with wisdom and compassion. Mindfulness also allows you to experience the richness of the present moment fully, enabling you to appreciate the beauty and wonders of life in its many facets.

C. Embracing Imperfection: The Beauty of Self-Discovery

In the journey of self-awareness, it's important to embrace

DECONSTRUCTING THE ENEMY

imperfection as a natural part of the human experience. Allow yourself the freedom to make mistakes, learn from failures, and grow from setbacks without self-judgment.

By accepting your imperfections and vulnerabilities, you can cultivate a deeper sense of authenticity and self-compassion. Recognize that your flaws and weaknesses are what make you unique and human, and that true growth comes from embracing and integrating all aspects of yourself.

Embrace the beauty of self-discovery as a lifelong journey of growth and transformation. By honing the sword of introspection, practicing mindfulness, and embracing imperfection, you can navigate the path to self-mastery with courage, grace, and a deep sense of inner peace.

As you continue on your journey of self-discovery, consider delving even deeper into the vast ocean of your inner world. Explore the depths of your subconscious mind through practices such as journaling, dream analysis, and meditation.

Journaling allows you to record your thoughts, feelings, and experiences in a structured manner, providing valuable insights into your innermost thoughts and emotions. By making a habit of journaling regularly, you can track patterns in your behavior, identify recurring themes, and gain a deeper understanding of your inner landscape.

Dream analysis is another powerful tool for unraveling the mysteries of your subconscious mind. Pay attention to the symbols, themes, and emotions present in your dreams, as they often provide valuable clues about your deepest desires, fears, and unresolved conflicts. By keeping a dream journal and reflecting on your dreams, you can uncover hidden aspects of your psyche and gain clarity on subconscious issues that may be influencing your waking life.

Meditation serves as a gateway to the silent realms of your inner being, allowing you to still the chatter of the mind and connect with your true essence. By practicing meditation regularly, you can cultivate a sense of inner peace, clarity, and awareness that transcends the noise of everyday life. In the stillness of meditation, you may discover profound insights about yourself and your place in the world, leading to a deeper sense of self-realization and spiritual connection.

As you delve deeper into the ocean of self, remember to approach this journey with an open heart and a spirit of curiosity. Embrace the unknown with courage and humility, knowing that the path to self-discovery is a sacred and transformative process that can lead to profound healing, growth, and self-acceptance.

A. Honing the Sword of Introspection

In the realm of introspection, we are confronted with the complexities of our inner landscapes, where the shadows of our past and the whispers of our fears reside. It is a sacred journey of self-exploration, a pilgrimage into the depths of our being where the fragments of our identities intertwine in a delicate dance of self-discovery.

As we bravely venture into the labyrinth of our thoughts and emotions, we encounter the echoes of our experiences, both joyful and painful. Through the reflective gaze of introspection, we unravel the narratives that have shaped us, peeling back the layers of conditioning and societal expectations to reveal the core essence of our true selves.

In the stillness of introspection, we forge a connection with our innermost desires and aspirations, listening to the whispers of our soul that beckon us towards paths unknown. It is a dance of vulnerability and strength, as we confront the shadows of our insecurities and fears with courage and compassion.

Through the practice of introspection, we cultivate a deep sense of self-awareness that becomes a guiding light in the darkness of uncertainty. We learn to navigate the ebbs and flows of life with a sense of clarity and purpose, grounded in the wisdom of our inner knowing.

As we continue to sharpen the sword of introspection, we embrace the paradox of being both fragile and resilient, vulnerable and powerful. It is in this dynamic tension that we discover the depths of our humanity, transcending the limitations of our past to embrace the boundless potential of our future selves.

In the sacred space of introspection, we find solace in the silence, where the cacophony of external expectations fades away, and we are left with the raw beauty of our authentic selves. It is a journey of self-acceptance and self-love, a testament to the courage it takes to confront our shadows and emerge reborn, like a phoenix rising from the ashes of our past.

In the tapestry of introspection, we weave the threads of our stories into a masterpiece of self-discovery and transformation. Through introspection, we come to understand that the true essence of our being lies not in the masks we wear or the roles we play, but in the uncharted territories of our souls that yearn to be explored and embraced.

As we delve deeper into the caverns of introspection, we encounter the fragments of our selves that have been long-buried beneath the layers of societal conditioning and external expectations. Here, in the depths of our inner world, we confront the shadows of our past traumas and fears, embracing them with a compassionate heart and a courageous spirit. It is in these moments of vulnerability and self-reflection that we unearth the gems of wisdom that have always resided within us, waiting to be discovered and embraced.

In the silence of introspection, we find a sanctuary where the noise of the external world fades into the background, and we are left with the gentle whispers of our inner voice guiding us towards our true path. It is a journey of integration and alignment, where we reconcile the disparate parts of ourselves and step into the wholeness of our being with grace and authenticity.

Through the practice of introspection, we cultivate a deep sense of self-compassion and self-love, recognizing that our imperfections and vulnerabilities are integral to our growth and evolution. We learn to dance with the shadows of our past without being consumed by them, embracing the full spectrum of our emotions and experiences with a sense of curiosity and gratitude.

As we continue to explore the caverns of introspection, we embark on a sacred quest to uncover the hidden treasures of our soul, recognizing that the journey towards self-discovery is an ongoing process of unraveling and rebirth. It is a pilgrimage of courage and resilience, where we navigate the twists and turns of our inner landscapes with a sense of curiosity and wonder, knowing that each step brings us closer to the truth of who we are meant to be.

In the boundless expanse of introspection, we find solace in the interconnectedness of all things, realizing that our individual journey is but a small part of the greater tapestry of existence. We embrace the interplay of light and shadow within us, honoring the duality of our human experience and finding beauty in the imperfections that make us uniquely whole.

B. Guardian of Your Thoughts: The Power of Mindfulness

In the intricate dance of life, our minds serve as both the conductor and the orchestra, orchestrating a symphony of thoughts, emotions, and perceptions. Mindfulness emerges as the guiding light, inviting us to step into the role of the guardian of our thoughts with grace and purpose.

At the core of mindfulness lies a profound invitation to bear witness to the marvels and complexities of our inner world. It calls upon us to cultivate a deep sense of presence, to anchor ourselves in the richness of each moment. Through the gentle art of mindfulness, we embark on a journey of self-discovery, exploring the depths of our consciousness with a sense of curiosity and wonder.

As we venture deeper into the realm of mindfulness, we begin to unravel the intricate patterns that shape our thoughts and beliefs. We come to realize that our minds are like vast oceans, teeming with currents of memories, fears, and desires. Through the practice of mindfulness, we learn to navigate these waters with skill and awareness, choosing to ride the waves of our thoughts with openness and discernment.

In the gentle embrace of mindfulness, we discover that our thoughts are not fixed entities but fleeting visitors passing through the landscape of our minds. With this newfound awareness, we can begin to untangle ourselves from the web of rumination and self-criticism, recognizing that our thoughts are but a small fragment of the vast mosaic of our being.

Mindfulness also offers us a mirror through which we can reflect upon the nature of our thoughts and emotions. By cultivating a nonjudgmental attitude towards our inner world, we create a safe space for self-exploration and growth. We come to understand that every thought, no matter how trivial or profound, carries with it a message, a lesson to be learned, a facet of our innermost self waiting to be revealed.

As we deepen our practice of mindfulness, we may find that the boundaries between ourselves and the world begin to blur. We become attuned to the interconnectedness of all things, sensing the subtle threads that bind us to each other and to the vast tapestry of existence. This awareness fosters a deep sense of compassion and empathy, as we realize that our joys and struggles are shared by all beings on this wondrous journey called life.

Being the guardian of our thoughts with mindfulness requires vigilance and dedication. In a world that clamors for our attention and energy, it is easy to be swept away by the relentless tide of distractions and obligations. Yet, in the sanctuary of mindfulness, we find refuge—a quiet oasis amidst the chaos, where we can retreat to nourish our spirit and renew our sense of purpose.

In the sacred space of mindfulness, we discover the power to shape our inner landscape, to cultivate a garden of peace and serenity within our hearts. By tending to the seeds of mindfulness with care and intention, we can create a life that is rich in meaning and purpose, filled with gratitude, wonder, and a deep sense of connection to ourselves and the world around us.

C. Embracing Imperfection: The Beauty of Self-Discovery

Many of us strive for perfection in all aspects of our lives, whether it be in our work, relationships, or personal endeavors. However, the pursuit of perfection often leads to feelings of inadequacy, self-doubt, and anxiety.

By embracing imperfection, we allow ourselves the freedom to make mistakes, learn from them, and grow as individuals. Imperfection is not a weakness but a reflection of our humanity. It is through our imperfections that we reveal our authenticity and vulnerability, connecting us more deeply with ourselves and others.

Self-discovery is a journey of exploration and acceptance of all facets of ourselves, including the imperfect parts. It is about uncovering our true essence and embracing our unique qualities and quirks. By embracing imperfection, we learn to appreciate the beauty of our flaws and shortcomings, recognizing them as integral parts of who we are.

Through self-discovery, we learn to let go of unrealistic expectations and societal pressures to be perfect. Instead, we cultivate self-compassion, self-acceptance, and self-love. We embrace our imperfections with open arms, knowing that they are what make us beautifully flawed and wonderfully human.

In the beauty of self-discovery lies the opportunity for growth, healing, and transformation. It is a process of peeling back the layers of self-limiting beliefs and societal conditioning to reveal our authentic selves. By embracing imperfection, we embark on a profound journey of self-discovery that leads to greater self-awareness, inner peace, and fulfillment.

Through the lens of imperfection, we discover the power of resilience and adaptability. Embracing imperfection allows us to navigate life's challenges with grace and courage, knowing that setbacks and failures are not signs of weakness but opportunities for growth.

Furthermore, embracing imperfection opens the door to creativity and innovation. When we let go of the need to be perfect, we give ourselves permission to think outside the box, take risks, and explore new possibilities. Imperfection fuels our creativity, allowing us to express ourselves authentically and bring forth unique ideas and perspectives.

Ultimately, embracing imperfection is an act of self-compassion and self-empowerment. It is a declaration of self-worth and self-love, honoring ourselves in all our imperfect glory. Through the journey of self-discovery and embracing imperfection, we unveil the beauty of our authentic selves and step into our full potential as individuals.

Embracing imperfection is not about settling for less or becoming complacent; it is about acknowledging that perfection is an unattainable ideal. It is about shifting our mindset from one of self-criticism to one of self-acceptance and self-love. When we embrace our imperfections, we embrace our humanity and all the richness and complexity that comes with it.

Moreover, embracing imperfection allows us to develop a sense of empathy and understanding towards others. When we are kinder to ourselves and embrace our flaws, we are more likely to extend that kindness and acceptance to those around us. Imperfection becomes a thread that connects us all, reminding us that we are all imperfectly perfect in our unique ways.

In the realm of relationships, embracing imperfection fosters deeper connections and intimacy. When we allow ourselves to be vulnerable and authentic, we invite others to do the same. Imperfection becomes a bridge that brings us closer to others, creating bonds based on genuine acceptance and understanding.

Embracing imperfection also teaches us the value of resilience and grit. When we face challenges and setbacks with a mindset of embracing imperfection, we cultivate the strength to persevere and overcome obstacles. Imperfection becomes a source of inner fortitude and empowerment, guiding us through life's ups and downs with courage and grace.

In conclusion, embracing imperfection is a powerful act

of self-discovery, self-acceptance, and self-compassion. It is through our imperfections that we find our true selves, connect authentically with others, and navigate life's challenges with resilience and grace. Imperfection is not something to be feared or avoided but celebrated as a window into our humanity and a path towards growth and transformation.

* * *

Bibliography

Anālayo, Bhikkhu. "The Potential of Facing Anger with Mindfulness." Mindfulness 9, no. 6 (August 4, 2018): 1966–72. https://doi.org/10.1007/s12671-018-1006-0.

"Brilliant Imperfection: Twitches and Tremors." Duke University Press EBooks, December 31, 2020, 19–20. https://doi.org/10.1515/9780822373520-006.

Enrico Pieranunzi. "The Aesthetics of Imperfection," January 1, 2021, 225–29. https://doi.org/10.5040/9781350106086.0035.

Greenberg, Mark T., and Joy L. Mitra. "From Mindfulness to Right Mindfulness: The Intersection of Awareness and Ethics." Mindfulness 6, no. 1 (January 13, 2015): 74–78. https://doi.org/10.1007/s12671-014-0384-1.

Kabat-Zinn, Jon. "The Liberative Potential of Mindfulness." Mindfulness, March 19, 2021. https://doi.org/10.1007/s12671-021-01608-6.

Maja Spener. "The Reliability of Subjective Measures of Consciousness." Oxford University Press EBooks, January 31, 2024, 114–26. https://doi.org/10.1093/oso/9780198867449.003.0006.

Rowan, John. "The Self-Awareness Movement—a Rebuttal." Self & Society 14, no. 4 (July 1986): 157–63. https://doi.org/10.1080/03060497.1986.11084779.

Scott, Chris. "The Self-Awareness Movement—a Critique." Self & Society 14, no. 4 (July 1986): 151–57. https://doi.org/10.1080/03060497.1986.11084778.

Shonin, Edo, and William Van Gordon. "The Lineage of Mindfulness." Mindfulness 6, no. 1 (August 5, 2014): 141–45. https://doi.org/10.1007/s12671-014-0327-x.

Silvia, Paul J., and Ann G. Phillips. "Self-Awareness without Awareness? Implicit Self-Focused Attention and Behavioral Self-Regulation." Self and Identity 12, no. 2 (March 2018): 114–27. https://doi.org/10.1080/15298868.2011.639550.

Van Gordon, William, and Edo Shonin. "Mindfulness: The Art of Being Human." Mindfulness 9, no. 2 (September 27, 2017): 664–66. https://doi.org/10.1007/s12671-017-0819-6.

Wheeler, Megan S., Diane B. Arnkoff, and Carol R. Glass. "The Neuroscience of Mindfulness: How Mindfulness Alters the Brain and Facilitates Emotion Regulation." Mindfulness 8, no. 6 (June 21, 2017): 1471–87. https://doi.org/10.1007/s12671-017-0742-x.

9

The Path to Liberation

In our quest for understanding the nature of the enemy, we often find ourselves trapped in mental chains that limit our perception and cloud our judgment. These chains are constructed from our fears, biases, and past experiences, binding us to a narrow view of the world and perpetuating the cycle of conflict and division.

To embark on the path to liberation, we must first recognize the existence of these mental chains and acknowledge their hold on our thoughts and actions. By shining a light on our internal barriers, we can begin to unravel the knots that keep us bound to destructive patterns of thinking and behavior.

Breaking free from mental chains requires courage and introspection. It demands a willingness to confront our fears and insecurities, to challenge our deeply rooted beliefs, and to embrace the discomfort of uncertainty. It is a journey of self-discovery and transformation, a process of shedding old layers of conditioning to reveal the truth and beauty that lie beneath.

As we untangle the web of our inner conflicts and confront the shadows that loom large in our minds, we begin to experience a sense of liberation and empowerment. We learn to release the grip of negativity and judgment, to embrace the freedom of forgiveness and compassion, and to cultivate a sense of inner peace and harmony.

The path to liberation is not easy. It requires dedication, patience, and a commitment to self-growth. It challenges us to face our deepest fears and insecurities, to confront the darkness within, and to emerge stronger and more resilient on the other side.

But the rewards of liberation are immeasurable. By breaking free from mental chains, we open ourselves to a world of infinite possibilities and potential. We learn to navigate life with grace and confidence, to embrace the journey with courage and resilience, and to live authentically and fully in the light of our true selves.

On this path to liberation, we find the strength to rise above adversity, the wisdom to navigate challenges with grace, and the courage to embrace the unknown with open arms. It is a journey of transformation and self-discovery, a process of healing and growth that leads us towards a brighter and more fulfilling future.

In breaking free from mental chains, we find our true power and agency. We become the masters of our own destiny, the architects of our own liberation, and the guardians of our inner peace and serenity. It is a journey worth taking, a path worth walking, and a transformation worth embracing with open hearts and minds.

As we continue on this journey of liberation, we delve deeper into our psyche, unraveling the complexities of our consciousness and confronting the shadows that reside within. We become attuned to the subtle intricacies of our thoughts and emotions, recognizing the patterns that have held us captive for so long.

Through this process of introspection and self-exploration, we unearth buried traumas and suppressed fears, shining a light on the darkest corners of our psyche. We confront the demons that lurk in the shadows, facing them with unwavering courage and resilience.

As we navigate this inner terrain, we cultivate a profound sense of self-awareness and acceptance, embracing all aspects of our being with compassion and understanding. We learn to honor our vulnerabilities and celebrate our strengths, weaving a tapestry of wholeness and authenticity.

In the depths of our contemplation, we discover the interconnectedness of all things, recognizing that our liberation is intertwined with the liberation of others. We extend a hand of empathy and compassion to those who are still bound by their mental chains, offering support and guidance on their own journey towards freedom.

Through this collective awakening, we forge bonds of solidarity and unity, standing together as beacons of light amidst the darkness. We embody the essence of resilience and transformation, inspiring others to break free from their constraints and embrace the boundless potential that lies within.

As we continue to walk the path of liberation, we emerge as radiant beings of love and empowerment, radiating our newfound wisdom and clarity to all who cross our path. We embody the essence of freedom and authenticity, shining brightly as living testaments to the transformative power of breaking free from mental chains.

A. Breaking Free from Mental Chains

Breaking free from mental chains involves a profound and complex inner journey towards liberation and self-transformation. It requires a deep dive into the innermost recesses of our psyche, where the roots of our limiting beliefs, fears, and negative thought patterns intertwine with the very fabric of our being.

To break free from these mental chains, we must embark on a relentless quest for self-discovery and introspection. This journey demands a courageous willingness to confront the shadows that lurk within us, to face the demons of self-doubt, insecurity, and self-criticism that have haunted us for far too long.

Self-awareness emerges as our guiding light in this arduous process. It beckons us to untangle the intricate web of conditioning that has ensnared our minds and hearts, inviting us to witness the ways in which these mental chains have shaped our thoughts, emotions, and actions.

As we delve deeper into the labyrinth of our inner world, we must challenge the very foundations upon which our limiting beliefs stand. We are called to question the legitimacy of the narratives that have defined our sense of self and reality, to dismantle the walls that confine our potential and limit our growth.

Breaking free from mental chains is not merely an intellectual exercise; it is an act of profound courage and resilience. It demands that we step into the unknown, to embrace the discomfort of uncertainty and the vulnerability of self-exploration, knowing that true liberation lies beyond our comfort zones.

Throughout this transformative journey, we must cultivate a compassionate and patient stance towards ourselves. We must offer ourselves grace and understanding as we navigate the twists and turns of inner healing, knowing that growth is a nonlinear process marked by peaks and valleys, triumphs, and setbacks.

Ultimately, breaking free from mental chains heralds a rebirth of the soul, a shedding of old skins to reveal the radiant essence that lies at our core. It is an awakening to our inherent worthiness and a reclaiming of our power to shape our lives with intention and authenticity. In embracing this journey of liberation, we pave the way for a life lived in alignment with our deepest truths and highest aspirations.

This process of breaking free from mental chains is akin to a metamorphosis, where the caterpillar must surrender to the cocoon's darkness before emerging as a butterfly. Similarly, we must surrender to the discomfort and uncertainty of self-discovery, trusting that our inner journey will lead us to a place of profound growth and liberation.

Through this process, we come to realize that our mental

chains are not fixed and immutable but rather products of our conditioning and past experiences. By shining the light of awareness on these deep-seated beliefs and fears, we can begin to unravel their grip on our minds and hearts, paving the way for new possibilities and expanded horizons.

Breaking free from mental chains also necessitates a willingness to let go of familiar but limiting patterns of thought and behavior. It requires us to challenge our comfort zones, to embrace the unknown with courage and openness, knowing that true transformation awaits on the other side of our fears and insecurities.

As we continue on this journey of self-liberation, we may encounter resistance and obstacles along the way. Old wounds may resurface, triggering emotions that test our resolve and strength. Yet, it is in these moments of challenge and discomfort that our capacity for growth and healing is truly tested, calling us to face our fears with compassion and resilience.

In breaking free from mental chains, we reclaim our agency and power to shape our own narrative, to author a new story that aligns with our deepest values and aspirations. We step into the role of the protagonist in our own lives, taking ownership of our thoughts, emotions, and actions with a newfound sense of purpose and clarity.

As we emerge from the shadows of our past and step into the light of self-awareness and authenticity, we discover a newfound sense of freedom and empowerment that transcends the limitations of our former selves. We stand tall and strong, liberated from the chains that once bound us, ready to embrace a future filled with limitless potential and infinite possibilities.

B. Embracing the Unknown with Courage

In life, we are often faced with the unknown, with uncertainty and unpredictability that can provoke fear and anxiety within us. It is natural to seek comfort in the familiar and the known, but true growth and transformation often lie on the other side of the unknown.

Embracing the unknown with courage requires a shift in mindset and perspective. It involves letting go of our need for control and certainty, and instead, cultivating a sense of curiosity and openness towards what lies ahead. It is about stepping into the discomfort of uncertainty and trusting in our own resilience and adaptability to navigate whatever challenges may come our way.

Courage is not the absence of fear, but rather, the willingness to act in spite of it. It is about facing the unknown with a brave heart and a steadfast resolve, knowing that we have the strength and resources within us to overcome whatever obstacles may arise.

Embracing the unknown with courage also means reframing our perspective on failure and setbacks. Instead of viewing them as signs of defeat, we can see them as valuable learning experiences that ultimately propel us forward on our journey of self-discovery and growth.

By embracing the unknown with courage, we open ourselves up to new possibilities and opportunities that we may never have imagined. We allow ourselves to dream big, to take risks, and to pursue our deepest passions with conviction and determination.

In the face of uncertainty, we can find a sense of empowerment and liberation in embracing the unknown with courage. It is through these moments of stepping into the unknown that we truly come alive, embracing the fullness of life with an open heart and a fearless spirit.

Venturing into the unknown requires a blend of vulnerability and strength, a willingness to journey into uncharted territories with an open mind and a resilient spirit. It demands that we confront our fears head-on, acknowledging their existence while not allowing them to dictate our actions or decisions.

Navigating through the unknown is not a linear path; it is a messy, unpredictable journey with twists and turns that test our resolve and push us beyond our comfort zones. It is in these moments of uncertainty and discomfort that we discover our true capabilities and strengths, tapping into reservoirs of courage and resilience we never knew we possessed.

Embracing the unknown also invites us to embrace impermanence and change, recognizing that life is a continuous process of evolution and growth. By releasing our attachment to specific outcomes and remaining open to the infinite possibilities that the unknown holds, we free ourselves from the constraints of fear and limitation.

Ultimately, embracing the unknown with courage is a profound act of self-discovery and self-empowerment. It is an invitation to trust in ourselves and in the unfolding of life's mysteries, knowing that whatever challenges lie ahead, we have the inner fortitude and resilience to navigate through them with grace and resilience.

Embracing the unknown with courage is not merely a one-time act but a continual practice of facing uncertainties with bravery and an open heart. It is a journey of self-exploration and self-mastery, where we learn to lean into discomfort and embrace the ebb and flow of life's ever-changing currents.

As we navigate the uncertain terrain of the unknown, we may encounter moments of doubt and fear, but it is in these moments that our true strength and courage are tested. It is in these moments of vulnerability that we find the resilience and tenacity to push forward, to embrace the challenges with a sense of resilience and determination.

The unknown holds within it the potential for greatness, for transformation, and for profound personal growth. When we release our attachment to the safety of the known and step boldly into the uncharted territory of the unknown, we give ourselves permission to evolve, to expand, and to awaken to the limitless possibilities that life has to offer.

Courage is not the absence of fear, but the willingness to move forward in spite of it. It is an acknowledgment of our inner strength and a commitment to facing the uncertainties of life with a spirit of resilience and optimism. By embracing the unknown with courage, we embark on a journey of self-discovery and transformation that has the power to shape our lives in ways we never thought possible.

C. Rising Above Adversity: The Triumph of the Spirit

In the face of adversity, the human spirit is tested in ways that often reveal the depths of our inner strength and resilience. Adversity presents itself in myriad forms - from personal struggles and setbacks to external circumstances beyond our control. It is during these challenging times that we are called upon to confront our fears, to navigate through uncertainty, and to find the courage to persevere.

Adversity is a universal experience that transcends cultural, social, and geographical boundaries. It does not discriminate based on age, gender, or background; rather, it is a fundamental aspect of the human condition that unites us in our shared vulnerability and capacity for growth. Whether it comes in the form of illness, loss, financial hardship, or relationship difficulties, adversity has the power to shake us to our core and challenge the very foundations of our identity.

While adversity may bring pain and suffering, it also offers an opportunity for growth and transformation. It is through facing our challenges with grace and resilience that we have the chance to cultivate qualities such as resilience, patience, and perseverance. Adversity can be a powerful teacher, guiding us toward a deeper understanding of ourselves and our place in the world.

The triumph of the human spirit lies in our ability to rise above adversity, to find hope and strength in the face of overwhelming odds. It is about harnessing our inner resources, drawing upon our values and beliefs, and staying grounded in the knowledge that we have the power to endure and overcome.

In the midst of adversity, it is essential to cultivate a mindset of resilience and optimism. By nurturing our strengths, practicing self-compassion, and maintaining a sense of purpose and direction, we can weather any storm that comes our way. Adversity, while challenging, can also be a catalyst for profound personal growth and transformation.

As we journey through life's trials and tribulations, it is important to remember that adversity is not a sign of weakness but a testament to our resilience and inner fortitude. When we face adversity with courage and perseverance, we emerge stronger, more compassionate, and more fully aligned with our true selves. The triumph of the spirit is not in avoiding challenges but in embracing them as opportunities for growth and self-discovery, for it is through adversity that we uncover the true depths of our strength and the limitless potential that lies within us.

* * *

Bibliography

"Being and Courage." Yale University Press EBooks, December 31, 2017, 1–31. https://doi.org/10.12987/9780300170023-002.

Crookston B, West J, Hall P, Dahle K, Heaton T, Beck R,

Muralidharan C Mental and Emotional Self-Help Technology Apps: Cross-Sectional Study of Theory, Technology, and Mental Health Behaviors JMIR Ment Health 2017;4(4):e45 URL: https://mental.jmir.org/2017/4/e45 DOI: 10.2196/mental.7262

Hareven, Tamara K. "Rising above Life's Disadvantage." Routledge EBooks, March 5, 2018, 191–218. https://doi.org/10.4324/9780429500572-8.

Lim, Soo Ping. "Courage and Conviction," August 26, 2019. https://doi.org/10.1142/11597.

Prestia, Angela S. "Leadership Courage: Embracing Change to Rebuild." Nurse Leader 21, no. 2 (June 2022). https://doi.org/10.1016/j.mnl.2022.05.013.

The Lancet. "Adversity in Childhood: How the Past Defines the Future." The Lancet 388, no. 10058 (November 2016): 2324. https://doi.org/10.1016/s0140-6736(16)32172-9.

Tillich, Paul. "3. Pathological Anxiety, Vitality, and Courage" In The Courage to Be: Second Edition, 64-85. New Haven: Yale University Press, 2000. https://doi.org/10.12987/9780300170023-004

Tillich, Paul. "5. Courage and Individualization (The Courage to Be as Oneself)" In The Courage to Be: Second Edition, 113-154. New Haven: Yale University Press, 2000. https://doi.org/10.12987/9780300170023-006

"Transitional Journeys and Contemporary Adversity": Bristol University Press EBooks, December 2, 2021, 37–59. https://doi.org/10.2307/j.ctv249sg1r.7.

Turner, Bruce R. "Rising above the Norm." CRC Press

EBooks, July 27, 2021, 72–107. https://doi.org/10.1201/9781003096047-4.

10

The Journey Within

In the depths of our being lies a tapestry of complexities and contradictions waiting to be unraveled. Each layer peeled back reveals a new facet of our true self, shedding light on the shadows that have cast doubt and confusion over our identity. It is within this sacred space of self-exploration that we come face to face with our fears, desires, and insecurities, confronting the raw essence of who we are.

As we navigate the labyrinth of our inner world, we may encounter parts of ourselves that we have long neglected or suppressed. These fragments of our past selves, buried beneath layers of conditioning and societal expectations, yearn to be acknowledged and integrated into the tapestry of our being. Embracing these forgotten aspects of ourselves with compassion and acceptance is the first step toward wholeness and self-discovery.

Meeting Your True Self in the Mirror

In the mirror of self-reflection, we confront the reflection of our true self—a being of infinite potential and boundless creativity. This mirror does not distort or deceive; it reveals the essence of who we are, stripped of masks and personas. Gazing into this mirror requires courage and vulnerability, as we confront both the light and dark aspects of our being.

As we peer into the depths of our own soul, we may be met with unsettling truths and uncomfortable revelations. Embracing these shadowy corners of our psyche with courage and compassion allows us to integrate them into the whole of our being, fostering a sense of wholeness and authenticity. The mirror reflects not just our flaws and imperfections, but our inherent worth and beauty as well.

Embracing the Wholeness of Being

Embracing the journey within is an act of self-love and self-acceptance, a testament to our willingness to explore the depths of our own soul and unearth the hidden treasures within. As we embrace the wholeness of our being, we cultivate a sense of inner peace and harmony that transcends the chaos and turmoil of the external world.

In this journey of self-discovery, we come to realize that we are more than the sum of our parts—that we are divine beings, capable of immense love, wisdom, and compassion. Embracing the wholeness of our being allows us to tap into our true potential and live authentically, guided by the light of our own inner wisdom.

As we embark on the journey within, may we embrace the unknown with grace and courage, trusting in the transformative power of self-discovery and the beauty of embracing our true selves.

Embracing the intricacies of our self requires a willingness to delve deeper, beyond the surface layers of our persona, and into the core of our being. It is in this profound exploration that we unearth the fragments of our identity that have been long forgotten or overlooked, shedding light on the complexities that make us who we are.

As we navigate this intricate tapestry of self-discovery, we may encounter aspects of ourselves that challenge our perceptions and beliefs, inviting us to confront our shadows with unwavering honesty and compassion. This journey of introspection is not for the faint of heart, as it demands a willingness to face our innermost fears and vulnerabilities with courage and grace.

The mirror of self-reflection serves as a portal to our true essence, holding up a mirror to our soul that reflects both the light and darkness within us. It is in this mirror that we witness the unfiltered truth of our being, stripped of pretense and facades, revealing the raw beauty and authenticity that lies at our core.

Embracing the wholeness of our being is a journey of self-acceptance and integration, a sacred dance of embracing all aspects of ourselves with love and understanding. It is through this process of self-discovery that we uncover the hidden gems of our soul, tapping into our innate wisdom and divine essence with humility and gratitude.

As we navigate the depths of our being with openness and curiosity, may we embrace the transformative power of self-discovery and allow ourselves to be guided by the inner light that illuminates our path towards wholeness and authenticity.

A. Unveiling the Layers of Self

In the exploration of self-discovery, we navigate the labyrinth of our inner worlds with a steadfast commitment to uncovering the essence of who we are beyond the surface layers of our identities. This profound journey demands a willingness to confront our deepest fears, insecurities, and vulnerabilities with unwavering courage and compassion.

As we delve into the recesses of our psyche, we may encounter the echoes of past traumas that continue to reverberate through our lives, shaping our beliefs, behaviors, and relationships in ways that may not always serve our highest good. By bravely exploring these shadowy corners of our being, we create the space for healing, transformation, and integration of the fragmented parts of ourselves.

Through the process of self-discovery, we strip away the masks we wear to conform to societal expectations or shield ourselves from perceived judgment, unveiling the raw, unfiltered truth of our authentic selves. This vulnerable act of revealing our true essence allows us to tap into the wellspring of our inner wisdom, intuition, and creativity, illuminating the path toward greater self-acceptance and self-love.

In the sacred silence of introspection, we are invited to listen deeply to the whispers of our souls, which carry the profound truths that have always resided within us, waiting patiently to be acknowledged and honored. As we cultivate a practice of self-reflection and self-awareness, we unearth the hidden gems of our unique gifts, passions, and purpose, aligning ourselves with our truest selves and stepping into our power with clarity and confidence.

The journey of self-discovery is an ongoing process of growth, expansion, and self-realization that invites us to embrace the fullness of our humanity – the light and the shadow, the joy and the sorrow, the beauty and the imperfection. By courageously embarking on this transformative odyssey, we awaken to the limitless possibilities that exist within us and forge a deep connection to the divine essence that resides at the core of our being, guiding us on our path of self-discovery and personal evolution.

B. Meeting Your True Self in the Mirror

As you stand before the mirror, what do you see reflected back at you? Is it merely a physical image staring back, or is there something deeper, something more profound waiting to be acknowledged and embraced? Meeting your true self in the mirror goes beyond superficial appearances; it is about confronting your inner self with honesty and vulnerability.

The mirror serves as a powerful metaphor for self-reflection and introspection. It is a tool that allows you to see beyond the surface and uncover the layers of your being. Take a moment to gaze into your own eyes and ask yourself: Who am I? What are my fears, desires, and dreams? What masks have I been wearing to shield my true self from the world?

Meeting your true self in the mirror requires courage and self-acceptance. It means confronting your insecurities and vulnerabilities, embracing your flaws and imperfections, and acknowledging the parts of yourself that you may have hidden or suppressed. It is a journey of self-discovery and self-love, where you come face to face with the essence of who you truly are.

As you engage in this process of self-confrontation, be gentle with yourself. Let go of self-judgment and criticism, and instead approach yourself with kindness and compassion. Recognize that the reflection in the mirror is a complex and multilayered individual, worthy of love and acceptance just as you are.

Meeting your true self in the mirror is an ongoing practice, a daily ritual of self-exploration and self-awareness. It is about peeling back the layers of conditioning and societal expectations to reveal the authentic self beneath. Embrace this journey with an open heart and a curious mind, allowing yourself to be vulnerable and authentic in your self-examination.

As you continue to meet your true self in the mirror, you may uncover aspects of yourself that surprise and challenge you. Embrace these discoveries with an open mind, for they are a testament to the depth and complexity of your being. Allow yourself to grow and evolve through this process of self-discovery, knowing that true liberation comes from accepting and embracing the entirety of who you are.

In the mirror of self-reflection, you will find not just a

physical reflection, but a reflection of your soul. Embarking on this journey will lead you to confront not only your past and present but also your future self, opening up a world of infinite possibilities and self-realization. Through this deep introspection, you will begin to unravel the mysteries of your inner world, uncovering deep-seated beliefs, traumas, and desires that have shaped your identity.

Embrace this profound journey with reverence and awe, for it is a sacred excavation of the self, a quest for truth and authenticity that will ultimately lead you to greater self-awareness and self-actualization. As you navigate the depths of your being through the mirror's reflection, remember to approach yourself with patience and grace, knowing that each revelation brings you closer to the core of your being and the essence of your true self.

The mirror, with its silent wisdom, offers a portal to the depths of your subconscious mind, a gateway to the hidden recesses of your soul. It reflects not only your physical form but also the essence of your being, capturing the nuances of your emotions, thoughts, and desires in its shimmering surface. Take a moment to consider the profound mystery of the mirror and its role in unveiling the truths that lie dormant within you.

As you continue your journey of self-discovery through the mirror's reflection, pay attention to the whispers of your inner voice, the subtle cues and signals that guide you towards a deeper understanding of yourself. Embrace the discomfort and uncertainty that may arise as you delve into the depths of your being, for it is through these challenges that true growth and transformation occur.

In the mirror's gaze, you may confront aspects of yourself that you have long ignored or suppressed - fears, insecurities, and unmet desires that have shaped your perception of the world and yourself. Embrace these shadows with courage and compassion, recognizing that they are a fundamental part of who you are and hold the key to unlocking your true potential.

Allow the mirror to be a sacred space for self-exploration and self-expression, a sanctuary where you can be fully present with yourself without judgment or expectation. Take the time to sit with your reflection, to engage in a dialogue with your true self, and to deepen your understanding of the complexities and contradictions that make you uniquely human.

As you journey deeper into the mirror's reflection, you may discover hidden reservoirs of strength, resilience, and wisdom that have been waiting to be embraced and acknowledged. Embrace these gifts with gratitude and humility, recognizing that they are a testament to your inner power and capacity for growth.

In the mirror of self-reflection, you will find not only your physical form but also the essence of your spirit, the essence of your true self that transcends time and space. Embrace this sacred communion with yourself, knowing that in the mirror's reflection lies the key to unlocking your deepest truths and stepping into the fullest expression of who you are meant to be.

C. Embracing the Wholeness of Being

At the core of embracing wholeness lies the profound recognition that each individual is a multifaceted being, composed of myriad experiences, beliefs, and emotions that collectively shape their identity. It is a journey of self-discovery and self-acceptance that transcends the boundaries of societal norms and expectations, delving into the depths of the human psyche to uncover the hidden treasures and shadowy corners that comprise the whole.

When we embrace wholeness, we confront the dichotomies within us - the delicate dance between light and darkness, strength and vulnerability, certainty and doubt. It is in acknowledging and integrating these contrasting forces that we truly come to appreciate the richness and complexity of our being. Embracing wholeness requires us to navigate the turbulent waters of our inner landscape with courage and compassion, diving fearlessly into the depths of our subconscious to unearth the hidden truths that lie dormant within.

As we journey deeper into the labyrinth of our psyche, we encounter the echoes of past traumas, the whispers of unfulfilled desires, and the yearnings of our unexpressed potential. Embracing wholeness necessitates a willingness to sit with discomfort, to confront the shadows that lurk in the recesses of our soul, and to weave together the fragmented pieces of our identity into a cohesive tapestry of self.

In the process of embracing wholeness, we cultivate a profound sense of interconnectedness with all beings and the world around us. We recognize that our individual journey towards wholeness is intimately intertwined with the collective evolution of humanity, and that our actions reverberate far beyond the confines of our personal sphere. This awareness fosters a deep sense of responsibility and stewardship towards the Earth and all its inhabitants, compelling us to act with integrity, empathy, and mindfulness in our interactions with the world.

Ultimately, embracing wholeness is a sacred act of self-love and self-discovery, a journey of integration and transformation that leads us to a place of inner peace and authenticity. It is a profound invitation to dive into the depths of our being, to embrace our inherent complexity and imperfections, and to emerge stronger, wiser, and more aligned with our true essence. In embracing wholeness, we not only nourish our soul but also contribute to the collective tapestry of human evolution, weaving a web of interconnectedness and unity that transcends all boundaries and divisions.

* * *

Bibliography

BELLIN, ZVI. "Meaning through Being: Reclaiming the Wholeness of Personal Meaning." The Journal of Humanistic Counseling 52, no. 2 (October 2013): 208–22. https://doi.org/10.1002/j.2161-1939.2013.00043.x.

Haywood, Russell. (2021). Systems and methods for self and social discovery.

Takagi, Isao. "Human Well-Being." Encyclopedia of the UN Sustainable Development Goals (Print), November 25, 2020, 524–24. https://doi.org/10.1007/978-3-319-95981-8_300088.

Higgins, Lee, and Lee Willingham. "Wholeness and Well-Being." Routledge EBooks, February 10, 2017, 108–28. https://doi.org/10.4324/9781315637952-7.

Koptie, Steven W. "Indigenous Self-Discovery: 'Being Called to Witness.'" First Peoples Child & Family Review 5, no. 1 (May 7, 2020): 114–25. https://doi.org/10.7202/1069068ar.

Leuenberger, Muriel. "Simulate Your True Self." Think 22, no. 64 (January 1, 2023): 35–38. https://doi.org/10.1017/s1477175623000076.

Redick, Kip. "Pilgrimage as Self-Discovery in an Ecological Community." Religions 14, no. 4 (March 23, 2023): 434. https://doi.org/10.3390/rel14040434.

Rudy, Rudy, Irvan Ricardo .N. Samosir, and Landa Kro Hutabarat. "SELF-DISCOVERY: PSYCHOANALYSIS of the FILM BOHEMIAN RHAPSODY (2018)." JURNAL BASIS 9, no. 2 (October 22, 2022): 133–44. https://doi.org/10.33884/basisupb.v9i2.5495.

Self-Study Group, The. "Storytelling as Self-Study: Exploring the Bildungsroman of Teacher Educators." LEARNing Landscapes 11, no. 2 (July 4, 2018): 345–53. https://doi.org/10.36510/learnland.v11i2.967.

Seto, Elizabeth, and Rebecca J. Schlegel. "Becoming Your

True Self: Perceptions of Authenticity across the Lifespan." Self and Identity 17, no. 3 (April 28, 2017): 310–26. https://doi.org/10.1080/15298868.2017.1322530.

Thakadipuram, Thomas. Leadership Wholeness, Volume 1. Palgrave Studies in Workplace Spirituality and Fulfillment. Springer International Publishing, 2023. https://doi.org/10.1007/978-3-031-08053-1.

www.ingramcontent.com/pod-product-compliance
Lightning Source LLC
Chambersburg PA
CBHW071719020426
42333CB00017B/2322